LEARNING TO READ IN CHINA

LEARNING TO READ IN CHINA
Sociolinguistic Perspectives on the Acquisition of Literacy

John E. Ingulsrud
and
Kate Allen

The Edwin Mellen Press
Lewiston•Queenston•Lampeter

LB
1577
.C48
I54
1999

Library of Congress Cataloging-in-Publication Data

Ingulsrud, John E.
  Learning to read in China : sociolinguistic perspectives on the
acquisition of literacy / John E. Ingulsrud and Kate Allen.
      p. cm.
  Includes bibliographical references (p.) and index.
  ISBN 0-7734-7961-9
  1. Chinese language--Study and teaching (Elementary)--China.
2. Reading (Elementary)--China. 3. Chinese characters--Study and
teaching (Elementary)--China. 4. Sociolinguistics.   I. Allen,
Kate. 1950- .   II. Title.
LB1577.C48I54   1999
372.4' 0951--dc21   99-30316
                                                                                      CIP

A CIP catalog record for this book is available from the British Library.

The Edwin Mellen Press	The Edwin Mellen Press
Box 450	Box 67
Lewiston, New York	Queenston, Ontario
USA 14092-0450	CANADA L0S 1L0

The Edwin Mellen Press, Ltd.
Lampeter, Ceredigion, Wales
UNITED KINGDOM SA48 8LT

Printed in the United States of America

Table of Contents

List of Figures and Tables

Figures

Tables

Appendix

Foreword

Nanjing, China was our home from 1988 to 1994. We worked in two universities there as Foreign Experts, teaching applied linguistics and the English language, and functioning also as teacher-educators. During the course of our stay, the Chinese language and its social meaning provided for us a constant source of fascination. While shopping in Shanghai, for instance, we noticed certain individuals not being helped by shop assistants. We further observed that the shop assistants attended to the customers who were speakers of Shanghainese and ignored the customers who were Putonghua (standard Chinese) speakers. What was the status of Putonghua in Shanghai? Wasn't Putonghua the language of prestige? In other instances, we were frequently stopped on the streets of Nanjing by travelers from out of town seeking directions. Although we both look unmistakably foreign, the genuine requests were made not in English, but in Putonghua. Why did they ask us?

We posed these questions to our graduate students in our linguistics courses. The students were unanimous in agreeing that Putonghua held the position of China's prestige variety. But they could not explain why speakers of Putonghua did not necessarily receive good service in Shanghai or why out-of towners would ask us for directions in Putonghua. We noticed, also, that most of our students did not attempt to speak Putonghua with standard pronunciation, even though they were fully capable of doing so, having learned to speak English with standard British pronunciation.

These issues led us further to ask how our students acquired Putonghua as children. Those students from areas where no form of Putonghua is spoken on the streets, insisted that learning Putonghua as a medium of instruction did not constitute a problem. Bearing in mind that fewer than one percent of all people in the People's Republic of China have access to higher education, perhaps our students, as part of that small elite group, were among those who did not have much trouble adjusting to the language of school. But is this the case for most children? With this question in mind, we went to the schools where we hoped we could observe first-hand children learning Putonghua.

We started out by making inquiries through the educational bureaucracy of Jiangsu Province, in October, 1989. Our contact person, a retired professor, suggested that our written request should be made by Kate Allen because her teaching post was at Nanjing University. This national university was regarded in the city as being more prestigious than Nanjing Normal University, a province-level university, where John Ingulsrud was teaching. It was not, however, until June, 1990 that we were finally given an appointment with Zhu Jialong of the Jiangsu Province Education Commission who is responsible for the promotion of Putonghua. Through his assistance, we were able to gain entry, the following September, to Changjiang Road School, a key elementary school for the city of Nanjing. They allowed us to observe the first-grade Chinese language class for the initial five weeks. During this time, children learned the romanized Hanyu Pinyin system. The school allowed us to come six days a week, but because of our own teaching schedules we could not come at the same time every day. We were able to observe a class each day and observe the process, with different teachers and different pupils. When the time came for Chinese characters to be introduced, we requested an extension of our observation. We were granted only one week.

Our observations produced a great deal of data. Early on, we became aware that the children who came to first grade already had a basic knowledge of Hanyu Pinyin and Putonghua in spite of what was said to the contrary by the Education Commission. To see whether this knowledge was due exclusively to family literacy, we attempted to gain entry to a kindergarten. Through our university connections, we were allowed to observe classes at Nanjing University Kindergarten, which confirmed to us that Hanyu Pinyin was indeed taught in kindergarten. From April to July in the final year, one hour of class per week was devoted to reading and writing Roman letters. We observed kindergarten children learning to read in the spring of 1991 and 1992.

The material we collected stimulated more questions, so we sought another opportunity to observe the same process at an elementary school, but this time with one teacher and one class. By now, we felt that we had exhausted our official connections. Before we attempted to explore other channels, an American friend of ours offered to introduce us to a teacher in a neighborhood school near where we lived. We observed her class at Yizhongxin School daily for six and a half weeks. When Chinese characters were being presented, we requested to extend our stay. Again we were asked to conclude the observation within a week.

Our data consist entirely of written notes of our observations. Classroom research today normally involves the video-taping of the classes being analyzed; however, both schools refused our request to video-tape. The teacher at the neighborhood school allowed us to audio-tape the class for a few days, but then decided against it. In these cases, we respected the wishes of the teachers. The reliability of our observations is based first on the fact that there were two of us observing, second, that the observations took place over a period of six weeks or more, and third, that the same process was observed in two different settings.

Still, the observation is subject to human perception filtered through the observer's frame of reference. John, having been born and raised in Japan, found his literacy skills in Japanese to be an asset in learning Chinese. John focused on the language of the classroom. Kate Allen, having returned to her native Zimbabwe after independence in 1981 as a teacher-educator, was acquainted with the issues of learning to read in a multilingual setting. Kate, in her observation, focused on classroom activity. We found this stereophonic approach useful. Although we discovered our notes turned out to be much the same, we also surprised each other on seeing things that the other missed. Each day after the observation, we returned home and exchanged information on what we saw and heard. Then we immediately entered our notes in our computers.

Gaining entry to the schools was not easy. It involved, on the one hand, careful planning using official channels. There were definite advantages to this approach. For example, our presence as foreigners in the school could not become a source of future problems for the teachers. We were "cleared," as it were, by the authorities. The problem with the official approach was the lack of rapport between the observers and the teachers. For instance, we did not feel free to speak to the teacher after class. The unofficial approach to gain entry, on the other hand, allowed us more informal access to the teacher and pupils. At the same time, there was a level of stress: What kind of trouble might we bring on this teacher, in view of China's recent history, for having allowed foreign researchers into her classroom?

Both official and unofficial approaches have been valuable for us in gaining entry to schools. In our experience, each approach provides a different quality of information. The official approach recognizes a nationally centralized bureaucratic system where officials on the provincial and municipal levels play a leading role. They and their contacts supplied us important institutional information. The unofficial approach provided us with informal contacts through which we could learn about the impact of school education on people at a personal level.

Preface

It may come as a surprise to readers of this book that young children in China begin learning to read in school with a Roman alphabet, Hanyu Pinyin, rather than with Chinese characters. I first discovered this approach in the fall of 1993, when I visited a first grade classroom in the city of Nanjing, where I was able to observe first-hand a teacher's lessons introducing Pinyin to the children. The classroom was crowded, the children were sitting in rows with their eyes trained on the teacher, and the teacher was directing them to answer her questions in chorus. It was, by western standards perhaps, a traditional, teacher-centered classroom. This classroom participation structure was not surprising to me, considering the immense task of educating so many children in overcrowded classrooms in the most populated country in the world, and considering that Chinese children are taught to listen carefully and emulate their elders. What did surprise me was that the children were getting their first reading lessons through the Pinyin alphabet.

I was told by the two researchers who had arranged my visit that it is not easy for foreign scholars to obtain permission to do long-term studies of Chinese primary classrooms. Those same researchers are this volume's authors, whose success in securing permission for extended observations of two first grade classrooms and a kindergarten in Nanjing, China are enough to grant the book a special place among other studies of Chinese language education. This work complements the portraits of Chinese children's literacy education reported by Chance (1989), who describes schooling in a Beijing commune largely through extensive interviews with parents, students and teachers, and by Parry (1998), who edited a volume in which Chinese teachers of College English recall their own childhood awakenings to literacy. In *Learning to Read in China,* we spend more time inside the classroom in the tradition of Marie Clay's (1967) pioneering study of young children's emergent literacy in New Zealand and Yetta Goodman's (1967) study of beginning readers in the U.S. In short, this detailed account of emergent literacy in Chinese classrooms is one that has not been told before.

What are children learning when they learn to read and write in Chinese at school? They learn a standard spoken language, two writing systems, romanized Pinyin and Chinese Characters, and they learn to "do" school-based literacy practices such as reading aloud, choral repetition, memorization, test-taking, repeated writing practice of both letter and character forms, and dictation. But readers will discover in these pages more than a description of how young children are taught to decode and write. We are led to look underneath these classroom practices at their historical, cultural, and political foundations as the authors take us step by step through the children's learning process. We come to find out that a major ideological goal in China is to maintain political unity through a common spoken and written language. We discover that achieving literacy in China means first learning the standard spoken language—Putonghua, literally the common language of the people. The authors explain that this is no mean feat, as children throughout China belong to different dialect groups. They pay particular attention to the Nanjing dialect, a non-standard form of Mandarin, the language variety that the children bring to the three classrooms we are learning about. This prepares us to understand the children's (and the teachers') process of adapting to the Putonghua pronunciation and helps us to follow the various methods used to teach the sounds and letters. Once children learn Pinyin, they begin to read and write simple sentences. After just six weeks, the children are introduced to Chinese characters, while continuing to use Pinyin. The alphabetic system is gradually phased out as the children begin the prolonged task of building a repertoire of character recognition and production. At this point the children are embarking on a tradition covering more than three thousand years of written text. It is through reading these texts that children will become socialized to be adult members of this nation and identify with its rich history and culture.

This volume adds to the mosaic of literacy practices, which Brian Street

(1995) argues that we need to create through case studies of many different social situations. In doing so, we can demonstrate how literacies around the world are saturated with specific cultural meanings and used for various ideological purposes. This book adds to the mosaic, showing how teaching practices associated with literacy reflect cultural norms and national policies and how learning to read in China is a complex and remarkable achievement.

Jo Anne Kleifgen

Teachers College
Columbia University

References

Chance, N. (1987). Chinese education in a village setting. In G. & L. Spindler (Eds.), *Interpretive ethnography of education at home and abroad* (pp. 221-246). Hillsdale, NJ: Laurence Erlbaum.
Clay, M. (1967). The reading behavior of five-year-old children: A research report. *New Zealand Journal of Educational Studies, 2,* 11-31.
Goodman, Y. (1967). *A psycholinguistic description of observed oral reading phenomena in selected young beginning readers.* Unpublished doctoral dissertation, Wayne State University, Detroit.
Parry, K. (Ed.). (1998). *Culture, literacy and learning English: Voices from the Chinese classroom.* New York: Heinemann.
Street, B. (1995). *Social literacies: Critical approaches to literacy development, ethnography and education.* New York: Longman.

Acknowledgements

This study was initially made possible by Professor Wu Zhanyun of Nanjing Normal University and Zhu Jialong of the Jiangsu Province Education Commission. They arranged the first opportunity for long-term observation in the classroom. Our second opportunity was made possible with the assistance of Ellyn MacInnis. We are grateful for these people's willingness to share their contacts. We would like to thank the teachers and administrators of Changjiang Road School and Yizhongxin School. We appreciate their patience for having us in their classes and their willingness to share their professional lives with us. Some of their names in the text have been changed. We also thank Yu Ningping for introducing us to Nanjing University Kindergarten. We thank the teachers there for allowing us to observe their classes. We would also like to thank the children in all of the classes we observed for sharing their experiences with us.

In the preparation of the manuscript, we thank Susan Offner, Paul Robins, and Li Dehua for their detailed and insightful editorial assistance. We also thank Miriam Black and Kevin Axton for their assistance. We thank Emi Mizutani, Miki Sakamoto, and Mari Ito of Kyushu Lutheran College Library for their assistance in procuring sources, as well as the staff of the libraries of the Chinese University of Hong Kong and the Nanyang Technological University in Singapore for allowing us access to their resources. Finally, any shortcomings in the book rest entirely with the authors.

1

Introduction

In the late summer of 1989, during those tense weeks after the violent suppression of the pro-democracy movement in Tiananmen Square, we moved across town. We were to change our residence from the campus of Nanjing Normal University to that of Nanjing University. Our new apartment was larger, but it was badly in need of paint. We requested the university authorities to have the apartment painted but they refused for budgetary reasons. They gave us permission to paint it at our own expense and engaged a private paint company to do the job for us.

The painters worked hard. Twice a day the boss, a woman who was about 60 years old, came to inspect the progress. We were impressed with the paint job when it was completed, and asked the boss for her name and address so that we could recommend her company to others. She hesitated, and after a few moments, confessed that she could not write. She then told us her name was Chen— *ěrduo* Chen (陈)—the character for Chen with the ear radical, not one of the other characters, including 成, 程, or 谌 that have similiar pronunciation. She described her name as it is written in Chinese characters and knew that there were several similar-sounding family names. She also knew enough about the construction of Chinese characters to know that the ear radical set her name apart from the others. After this explanation, she dictated her address to us.

A few months later, when we met Ms. Chen on the street, we noticed she was wearing a gold ring. When we ran into her at other times in the next year or two, she was wearing gold earrings and a gold necklace. There was no doubt that Ms. Chen was a successful business woman. She had made the economic boom of Eastern China work for her and did so with minimal literacy skills. The success of Ms. Chen and others like her have raised questions about the value of education, especially in terms of profit-making.

The answer to the question: Why learn to read? tends to be treated as a self-evident one. Educators and politicians alike see reading and writing as necessary skills for citizens to function in a modern society. For instance, the full participation in the democratic process requires literacy skills. For a society to excel in science and technology requires a population who can read and write. Moreover, the preservation of civilization, as well as its further development, is made possible by the activities of reading and writing. Yet, in spite of the lofty arguments for the acquisition of literacy, we pose this basic question at the outset of our study. Our observations of Chinese society today lead us to believe that acquiring literacy is not a self-evidently worthwhile venture for the individual.

The discourse of literacy has tended to construct the phenomenon as an either/or entity, that people are either illiterate or literate. More realistically, literacy is a continuum with people possessing varying degrees of literacy (Barton, 1994). Problems arise in defining what degrees or levels constitute literacy. There are general terms like "semi-literate," which refers to people who read and write with difficulty. "Aliterate" refers to people who, having learned to read and write, simply do not use the skills. The term most often used is "functionally literate," a category used by international organizations like the United Nations Education, Scientific, and Cultural Organization (UNESCO) in compiling data on literacy. A functionally literate person can: "engage in all those activities in which literacy is required for effective functioning of his group and community and also for enabling him to continue to use reading, writing, and calculation for his own and the community's development" (Harris & Hodges, 1995, p. 90). The UNESCO definition of a literate person, according to a document published in 1978, is one "who can with understanding both read and write a short simple statement on his every day life" (p. 90). While these definitions serve to describe levels of literacy, they do not help in quantifying or assessing literacy. In response to this issue, Vincent Greaney (1996, p. 16) quotes a more recent 1990 UNESCO document stating that basic literacy is indicated by "the completion of four grades of primary education," thus allowing a more quantifiable definition. Defining literacy in terms of school-based literacy raises further questions. There are examples both of schools failing to provide individuals with adequate literacy skills and of the home environment successfully providing literacy skills without school intervention. The fact that the number of years in school is used as a measure of literacy makes the study of school literacy more urgent. It is only through such studies that we know what is going on in the classrooms, and therefore what the statistics might mean.

In traditional China, literacy was linked to social and economic status. The scholar, particularly the one who passed the rigorous imperial civil service examinations, stood at the pinnacle of social achievement. Not all men in traditional China acquired literacy for this purpose. There were also practical reasons that would enhance the economic life of the family. If a person had access to education, varying degrees of opportunities for social mobility existed.

Moreover, in traditional Chinese society, as well as in the traditional societies of Japan and Korea, literacy meant being literate in classical texts. By becoming acquainted with the leading ideology of society—in East Asia's case, Confucianism—the literate person is seen to take on a higher moral character. Even for those who had access to limited education, the texts for reading were often of a moral nature (Rawski, 1979). Literacy, then, is not viewed simply as a practical skill. The mastery of reading and writing itself, because of the accompanying exposure to moral teachings, elevates an individual to a higher ethical plane. While people of letters may enjoy social prestige, they also bear the responsibility to act morally; therefore the conduct of a literate person is under greater scrutiny.

Chinese society in the 1990s does not draw on a single cultural tradition, in spite of the scholarly legacy of over 3000 years. A number of social upheavals in the nation's recent history have fostered perspectives that run contrary to traditional views. Despite the upheavals earlier in this century, namely, the fall of the imperial dynasty, weak republican government and warlordism, and the subsequent invasion by the Japanese, it is the events within the tenure of the Communist regime since 1949 that have shaken society to its core. The Great Leap Forward in 1957 collectivized both rural and urban society, thereby destroying many traditional institutions and stamping out most forms of dissent. The Cultural Revolution from 1966 to 1976 not only challenged ancient customs, but those basic values of relationship that held families and friendships together. Children denounced

4

parents. Friends informed on each other. The breakdown of values that promoted social cohesion has provided fertile ground for the individualistic pursuit of monetary wealth in recent years.

It is into this competing arena of values that young school children are thrust. There they encounter the Confucian tradition that exalts learning, the Communist ideology that promotes service to society, and the popular feeling that what counts in the end is money. Surrounded by these values, school children attend to the task of learning to read and write in standard Chinese. The study of Chinese writing exposes children to the literary traditions of Confucian East Asia. As literate citizens, they are better prepared to work for the greater good of society. As speakers of standard Chinese who are proficient in Roman and Chinese scripts, they may possess more options in making money than those people without these skills.

Speakers of the Chinese language constitute at least one fourth of all human beings on earth.[1] In the People's Republic of China, where the vast majority of Chinese language speakers live, a nationwide effort is under way to teach the population to read. Although the government is attempting to provide elementary school education for all Chinese children, it is the children living in cities who receive the most benefit. All of them have access to nine years of education before they are weeded out by entrance examinations. In contrast, children living far from urban centers or in remote areas are considered fortunate if they can attend six years of school. It is estimated that approximately 74% of China's population (Bennett, 1996, p. 359) live in non-urban areas. That means rural children make up the vast majority. The availability of educational opportunities is largely dependent on the local area's economic strength. This is because most rural schools are locally funded (Robinson, 1986, 1991). Although the economic reforms begun in the late 1970s benefited the rural areas initially, later on these reforms brought more prosperity to the cities. Urban dwellers have had better access to education all along, so the added economic boost has exacerbated the gap between rural and urban China. To address this issue, the government has launched an ambitious

---

[1] It is estimated that the population of China in 1992 stood at 1,165,771,000. The percentage of the population that identifies itself as part of the Han nationality is 92%. We can then estimate that at least 1,072,509,320 people speak a variety of the Chinese language (*China facts & figures annual*, p. 88).

program to promote nine years of compulsory education in poor rural areas ("China Starts," 1996).

Learning to read in Chinese is no small feat. By sixth grade, or the end of elementary school, children should be able to read between 2500 to 3500[2] Chinese characters. While these figures provide a goal for the syllabus, numbers do not describe the kind of literacy that is achieved. Basic literacy is 1500 characters while the number needed for general use is between 3500 and 4000 characters (Taylor & Taylor, 1995). The situation is further complicated because some reading material is written in simplified characters and other material is written in the older complex characters. Furthermore, one can question whether adults who memorized a large number of Chinese characters in school are able to maintain that level of literacy throughout their adult life.

In China, literacy training in schools has an additional function. Children begin to read by learning the sounds and words of the standard language. As is described in chapter three, the reading lessons are conducted much like foreign language lessons. Children learn to speak standard pronunciation at the same time as they learn to read. Although it is possible to learn the Chinese characters in their own vernacular, children are required to learn them in the sounds of the standard language. Therefore access to literacy in China is channeled through (or limited to) the standard language. This added task of learning to speak the standard language, particularly for children who do not speak the standard at home, puts many Chinese children in a similar position to children in post-colonial societies who attend schools taught through the medium of a European language.

The teacher's task is no less complex. To start with, the teacher's social position is in a state of flux. Teachers, during the Cultural Revolution, lived under suspicion. Their acquaintance with many different ideas was thought to detract from their commitment to the common cause of building up socialism. Divisions emerged between teachers who were more zealous and those who were less zealous. The legacy of those ten years is still felt in the schools. Today, persecutor and victim continue to live and work side by side. Teachers, who are considered intellectuals, complain that they have not recovered the status the Confucian world

---

[2]This figure is provided by Zhu Jialong of the Teaching Research Office of the Jiangsu Province Education Commission, personal communication, 1990. See chapter five for a more detailed discussion.

view would ascribe to them, in spite of their rehabilitation since Deng Xiaoping initiated the age of 改革开放 *gǎigé kāifàng* 'reform and opening to the outside world.' They are challenged by another competitor—money. Teachers are often ridiculed as being unworldly, unenterprising, and poor. By becoming teachers, individuals have accepted fixed salaries and a life with few economic benefits. Indeed, only a small number of our university students selected education as a career when they had a choice.

Despite the negative press the teaching profession in China has received, this study documents conditions of teachers that are not as lamentable as is often described in China and abroad. Teachers, we have observed, do have access to power in society. They do have ways to increase their income and find ways to be part of the mainstream economy. Teachers can rise to positions of influence.

The teacher's professional task is demanding. The task of the elementary school teacher, for example, involves (a) negotiating the differing varieties in the Chinese speech community, (b) managing large classes of more than 50 pupils who are almost all only children, (c) teaching children to speak the standard language, and (d) teaching Chinese characters through the medium of a romanized alphabet.

In this study, we document the process children and teachers go through in schools, beginning with learning to read up to the introduction of Chinese characters. Our purpose is to understand the nature of this process. In 1980, Michael Stubbs argued for a need for observational studies on the acquisition of literacy in specific contexts including the classroom: "Very few studies are based on direct classroom observation of children actually learning to read and write in real lessons" (p. 163). His assertion is still relevant. Putting the context of China in perspective, more children engage in acquiring literacy through the process we describe than in any other literacy acquisition process in the world.

Reading in the Chinese language, however, is not an unresearched area. The issue has been approached through a number of disciplines and many of the results have been published in the English language. There are studies on orthographies describing the particular nature of each system and the cognitive processes needed to comprehend and remember them. There are studies on the Chinese educational system, the schools, and the curricular contexts in which literacy is a major component. There are studies that describe reforms in language and education and the motivations to implement the measures.

Chinese writing has long been of interest to scholars because it represents an unbroken civilization, and it employs a non-alphabetic system. European fascination, often motivated by the desire to engage in evangelistic work, has resulted in descriptions of Chinese writing. These descriptions go back to Christian missionaries in the sixteenth century, most notably, the Jesuits (e.g., Serruys, 1962; Spence, 1984). In the twentieth century, missionaries continued their efforts in describing the Chinese writing system (e.g., Wieger, 1927/1965; Mathews, 1943).

In addition to the work done by missionaries, other linguistic scholars such as Bernhard Karlgren (1923/1991; 1929) have provided extensive descriptions of the Chinese language and its writing system. More recently for instance, Jerry Norman (1988) has described Chinese writing in the context of the many varieties of Chinese speech. Robert Ramsey (1987), in a similar kind of description, includes the languages of many ethnic minorities in China. Other descriptions have taken an evaluative view, arguing that because the Chinese writing system is so difficult to master, with the resulting problems of promoting literacy, it should be replaced by an alphabetic alternative (e.g., DeFrancis, 1984; Hannas, 1997). Further descriptions compare Chinese writing to other writing systems. Insup Taylor and Martin Taylor (1995) compare the writing systems of Northeast Asia. Florian Coulmas (1989) examines Chinese writing together with other major writing systems of the world.

Many of the studies above refer to a body of research employing methods of cognitive psychology to explore the nature of recognition and comprehension of different orthographic systems. These kinds of studies have been primarily carried out in North America, Japan, Taiwan, and Hong Kong (e.g., Chen & Tzeng, 1992; Iwata, 1984; Kao & Hoosain, 1986; Tzeng, Hung, & Garro, 1978; Tzeng, Hung, & Wang, 1978; Yamadori, 1988). In these studies, speeds of comprehension and visual perception have been measured, as well as hemispherical processing. Some studies seriously question the existence of cognitive processes unique to specific writing systems, such as Chinese characters and Roman alphabets (e.g., Fang, Horng, & Tzeng, 1986; Seidenberg, 1985).

The research in writing systems provides information on the nature of the written language and the cognitive processes involved in acquiring it. Other studies describe writing systems in terms of language policy, often involving literacy issues (e.g., C. Cheng, 1985; Serruys, 1962; Seybolt & Chiang, 1979; Wu Yuzhang, 1958; Yin & Baldauf, 1990; Zhou Youguang, 1986). These works include compilations and analyses of official documents. Similar studies have been conducted on educational policy (e.g., Brown, 1986; Hawkins & Stites, 1991; Hu & Seifman, 1976; Lewin, Xu, Little, & Zheng, 1994; Rawski, 1979; Sidel, 1982). In view of the difficulty in obtaining information on social sciences in China, these works provide an important asset to research.

Although key documents, official and historical, are made available by these works, there are few studies that provide first-hand information reporting how language and educational policy is implemented. There is a small but growing volume of work that describes reading experiments conducted in Chinese schools (e.g., Dai & Lu, 1985; Shu & Anderson, 1997). Other studies employ various observational techniques to describe learning in schools, though not specific to literacy (e.g., Tobin, Wu, & Davidson, 1989; Weber, 1979). Although a number of studies describe the literacy policies for Chinese children, we are unaware of any research informing how these policies are actually implemented in schools. Our intention is to provide information on how school literacy is carried out.

To describe the literacy acquisition process in schools and the significance of this process, we have arranged the book thematically. Learning to read, in reality, is not a neatly compartmentalized process. Literacy involves a number of contexts and skills operating simultaneously. A narrative might be most faithful to this reality; however, we have chosen a thematic approach to assist readers who may be interested in particular literacy skills. At the same time, we do not understand the acquisition of literacy to occur in a vacuum. We believe that the manner in which it is done relates to a particular history and specific kinds of institutional settings. In chapters one and two, we describe the historical and social contexts in which literacy acquisition takes place. In chapters three, four, and five, we examine the task of acquisition. In chapters six and seven, we interpret the task in the light of historical and social forces.

We begin in chapter one by describing the linguistic context of China. Here we argue that the task for Chinese children of learning to read, and specifically children in the city of Nanjing, is a sociolinguistic one involving the appropriate use of regional and standard language varieties and learning the differences between written and spoken language. We provide the historical background of the choice for a standard language and the choice of an alphabetical system that represents the standard language, as well as the politics of language reform. In chapter two, we describe the institutional and social contexts. The two schools where we observed classes, the key school and the neighborhood school, are compared and contrasted in terms of the kind of student body, facilities, and the manner in which they are funded. We describe the life of the teachers: their professional life, their relationship with parents, and their changing status in society. The role of preschool education in the acquisition of literacy is also considered.

In chapter three, the description of the classroom activities begins. We focus first on speech, and document how the standard language, Putonghua, is taught. We describe the developmental and dialect-based difficulties the children have as they learn to speak standard Chinese. In chapter four, we focus on the process of learning the Roman letters of Hanyu Pinyin. We document the process of learning letter-shapes and the morphological problems of connecting syllables to words. In chapter five, we describe the transition from Hanyu Pinyin to Chinese characters. We document the difficulties children meet in the initial adjustment to Chinese characters. Furthermore, we analyze how literacy skills at this stage are assessed.

In chapter six, we discuss our findings in terms of various kinds of literacy. We review the task of acquiring literacy in China and suggest the motivations for the particular manner in which it is done. In chapter seven, we summarize our findings and interpret them in the light of global issues of literacy.

In the text, we provide terms in Chinese in both romanization and Chinese characters. At the first occurrence of a term, we provide the Hanyu Pinyin rendition with tone diacritics together with current simplified forms of Chinese characters. For subsequent occurrences, the terms are provided in Hanyu Pinyin without tone diacritics. For terms that are specifically associated with Imperial China and the Republic of China, we provide the Chinese character renditions in the older complex forms. In certain cases we also provide a Wade-Giles transcription of a term as well. In cases describing non-standard pronunciation, the International Phonetic Alphabet (IPA) is used for transcription. For assistance in deciphering the IPA, and Hanyu Pinyin and Wade-Giles romanization, please consult Tables A1 and A2 in the Appendix. The English examples provided are only approximations and readers should not draw precise phonetic conclusions from them. By reading the text, we hope that the reader will recognize the orthographic complexity of the Chinese language.

Chapter One
Language and Literacy in China

Conventional linguistic terminology has inadequately described the multilingualism of China. 92% of the population make up the Han Chinese ethnic majority (*China facts & figures annual*, p. 88), and this largest ethnic group in the world could claim to speak the Chinese language. The remaining 8% include the Tibetan, Uighur, Mongolian, and Manchurian ethnic and linguistic minorities as well as numerous other groups. Of the billion or so people who consider themselves speakers of Chinese, including the ethnic minorities who speak Chinese, many speak a variety that is understood only in their locality or region. If we use "intelligibility," the extent to which a speech variety can be comprehended, as a definition for a language, the speakers of Chinese speak a number of languages. Consequently, the Chinese speech community can be characterized as a multilingual one. The situation, however, is not so simple. There are factors other than intelligibility, such as script, textual traditions, and national standards for speech that provide degrees of cohesion—enough cohesion to give the impression that most of the varieties are part of the same language, despite the actual diversity.

The major linguistic divisions of the Chinese language are indicated on the map below:

12

Figure 1. The linguistic map of China. The major dialect groups are indicated along with selected cities.[1]

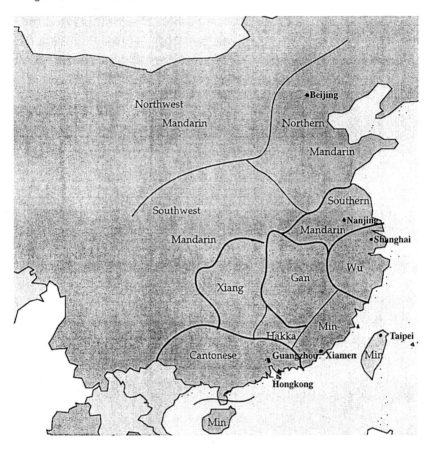

China is divided into two primary linguistic areas: North of the Yangzi River and the southwest of China on the one hand, and south of the Yangzi on the other. In the north and to the southwest, people speak varieties related to Northern Chinese or Mandarin Chinese. About 70% of the Han Chinese speak this general variety. Within Northern Chinese, there are three roughly mutually intelligible groups:

---

[1] The map was prepared with the software *Maps 'n facts* (1994) and additional reference to three sources: Huang (1987), Norman (1988), and Ramsey (1987).

Southwest Mandarin, Northern Mandarin, and Southeast Mandarin. The relative linguistic uniformity of the north and west is in marked contrast to south of the Yangzi River where the six major dialect groups exist: the Wu, Cantonese, Xiang, Min, Hakka, and Gan. Speakers of these varieties have reported to us that some of the dialects within these groups are non-intelligible. For example, our students from Jinhua in southern Zhejiang Province in the Wu-speaking area cannot understand speakers from coastal Wenzhou, also in the same Wu-speaking province.

Geographically, southern China is mountainous and receives regular rainfall. The agricultural societies in these hills and valleys tend to be stable and self-reliant with little population movement. In contrast, the plains of North China, prone to floods, drought, and invasions, have witnessed periodic movements of the population, which, according to Robert Ramsey (1987), allowed the language north of the Yangzi River to develop in a more uniform manner.

Popularly, the term "dialect," as well as the Chinese term *fāngyán* 方言, has been used to describe all varieties of Chinese whether they are intelligible or unintelligible. John DeFrancis (1984) points out that *fāngyán* technically means 'regional speech' and is distinct from *dìfānghuà* 地方话 meaning 'local speech.' To account for this sociolinguistic situation, he suggests that the eight large mutually unintelligible varieties be called "regionalects" and to ascribe "dialects" to the mutually intelligible varieties within each of the regionalects. We have chosen a more traditional categorization, that of Jerry Norman (1988) and Robert Ramsey (1987), who name the larger categories of the Chinese language as "dialect groups." The dialect groups are listed below with their respective population percentages (Ramsey, p. 87).

14

Table 1

Population Percentages of Dialect Group Speakers

Dialect Group	Percentage of Han Chinese Population
Mandarin (three northern groups) 北方话	71.5%
Wu 吴	8.5%
Cantonese 粤	5.0%
Xiang 湘	4.8%
Min 闽	4.1%
Hakka 客家	3.7%
Gan 赣	2.4%

Obviously, the Northern Chinese dialect group is the most dominant as far as numbers of speakers are concerned. The Northern group covers a large area from northeast China (Manchuria) to Yunnan in the southwest. Although this would seem a logical reason for choosing a standard language based on the Northern dialect group, political reasons also influenced the decision, especially concerning the choice of a specific variety for a standard.

The Development of Putonghua

A standardized variety of spoken Chinese is a relatively recent development. The written language of China has been more or less standardized for more than 2000 years. In 200 BC, under the first Qin emperor, the Chinese characters that have been in use through to the present time were standardized (Fairbank, 1992). Since Chinese characters possess a semantic component (as well as a phonological one), readers who could not speak the language of the capital could still, to a large extent, comprehend the meaning of government documents. Consequently, the Chinese characters were and are still seen as a common writing system for all varieties of Chinese and a unifying force in the culture. Even so, many people in the nineteenth century began to feel that for a modern nation to function, a standard spoken language was needed. Common speech would promote immediate and direct communication, facilitating both governmental control and economic development. It was felt it would also provide a sense of participation in the nation if the population spoke the same language.

The present Beijing area was first used as an imperial capital under the Liao dynasty in 907. Subsequently, it was also used by the Jin, Yuan, Ming, and Qing dynasties, and consequently, the speech of this area took on a special significance (Zhang Xiruo, 1955/1979). Since the emperor resided in Beijing, the city served as the center for government. The Mandarin variety of Chinese drew on the local version of Northern Chinese spoken in the city and was called *guānhuà* 官話 'speech of the mandarins.' Because this variety became the language of the power center, it maintained a great deal of prestige even when Beijing ceased to serve as the national capital during the Republican period (1927-49).

In this century, there have been several attempts to construct a standard language that reflected less the speech of government officials and more the speech of the common people. Some reformers attempted to construct a language that drew elements from each of the major dialect groups. The problem with the constructed varieties was that there was no one who spoke them natively. These languages also lacked the cultural motivation for people to try to learn them, because unlike modern speakers of Hebrew in Israel, who learned to speak an ancient written language, there was no historical evidence for the existence of these varieties. When the Communists took control of China in 1949, they, like their Nationalist predecessors, simply adopted Mandarin Chinese as the foundation for their standard language.

Mandarin Chinese, since it was based on the dialect of the imperial capital, was not acceptable to many reformers because it was not really a "people's language." However, to play down its elitist past, the new mandarins rechristened the dialect. The Nationalists called it *guóyǔ* (kuoyü) 國語 'national language,' and the Communists called it *pǔtōnghuà* 普通话 'common language.' Very little was changed. Even today, Putonghua on the mainland differs only slightly from Guoyu, the Mandarin Chinese of Taiwan.

Today Putonghua is the exclusive language of the media, heard on TV and the radio on the Chinese mainland. Even in major dialect group centers such as

Shanghai and Guangzhou (Canton), all the broadcasts are given in Putonghua, although the people of Guangzhou are also able to receive Cantonese broadcasts from Hong Kong. In Taiwan, Guoyu is used predominantly in the media. Taiwanese, a variety of the Min dialect group, is used in TV programs and the radio, but its share is much smaller than that of Guoyu.

When TV or film directors in the People's Republic of China need to use a regional variety for dramatic effect, the choice is almost always the Beijing city dialect. It is as if Brooklynese were the only sanctioned broadcast regional dialect in English. Regional speech, however, is heard when government leaders speak or when local people speak in interviews. When the interviewee's speech deviates too much from Putonghua, subtitles in Chinese characters are provided. Although most TV broadcasts in Taiwan contain subtitles in contrast to broadcasts on the mainland, we have noticed that broadcast Putonghua, on the mainland is spoken at a slower pace than Taiwan's broadcast Guoyu. However, the broadcast Putonghua is still spoken too quickly for some people. The Hong Kong newspaper, *The Standard*, reported that the then senior leader Deng Xiaoping complained that news reporters on TV were speaking too quickly ("Deng Tells," 1993).

Does the ubiquitous presence of Putonghua in the media mean that the southern dialect groups are in retreat? Jerry Norman (1988) presents examples where Putonghua vocabulary has been borrowed by the dialects, in particular the Wu dialect group of which Shanghainese is a part. Y. R. Chao (1968) presents examples of borrowings between dialect groups including varieties of Mandarin Chinese. In chapter three of this study, we present documented examples where Wu dialect pronunciation and Wu dialect vocabulary enter even the Putonghua lessons in Nanjing schools.

In spite of the efforts by the media and the schools to promote Putonghua, both the Southern dialect groups and non-standard Mandarin Chinese varieties persist. Chinese people in most areas, therefore, use at least two language varieties. These two varieties may be relatively similar in nature for some yet very dissimilar for others. Sociolinguists, such as Charles Ferguson (1959), have called this kind of linguistic situation diglossia. In a diglossic situation the two language varieties do not have equal value. One is a "high" variety which has more prestige and the other is a "low" variety. It is the standard language, and in China's case, Putonghua, which is the "high" variety and it is the local variety which is the "low" one. Another reason why the "low" varieties are often called dialects is that they lack the prestige needed for a full-fledged language (Haugen, 1966). The existence of a diglossic situation does not necessarily mean that "low" varieties will eventually disappear (Fishman, 1966). The presence of diglossia can be further explained by factors of prestige, power, and solidarity (e.g. Brown & Gilman, 1960; LePage, 1964; Pride, 1971).

For our purposes here, the notions of "prestige" and "solidarity" may be most helpful in describing the Chinese diglossic situation. Normally, speakers motivated by social mobility would try to emulate the standard variety for reasons of prestige. Others, to maintain certain group memberships, would speak non-standard varieties to express solidarity. Sometimes the motivation for group memberships may be similar to aspirations for prestige; however, we would like to ascribe the motivation for "prestige" to a regional or national identity that goes beyond identity to one's own locality. The motivation for "solidarity" would be ascribed to more localized or socially-marked identities. As Robert LePage and Andre Tabouret-Keller (1985) point out, the choices speakers make for using a language variety are acts of identity.

In the diglossic situation of China, the standard language, Putonghua, may not enjoy the status of an exclusive prestige variety. Although political power has generally been centered in Beijing for almost a thousand years, the North China Plain has not been the center of China's economy for the same length of time. The center of the economy has been the rich Yangzi River delta region, the area of the Wu dialect group. The Nationalists, in choosing Nanjing as their capital, did so with good reason. The city lay near China's most prosperous region. Since the late 1970s when the policies of "Reform and Opening to the Outside World" began to be implemented, the Eastern seaboard, particularly the Southeast, has experienced the fastest pace of economic growth. The dialect group-speaking cities of Shanghai, Xiamen, and Guangzhou have all outpaced the cities to the north and west. In Beijing, it is trendy to use Cantonese words. For example, the transliterated Cantonese word 的士 [dəksi] is used for 'taxi,' but often with the Putonghua pronunciation of the Chinese characters: *dīshì*. Other examples include *dǎdī* 打的 'hail a taxi' and *miàndī* 面的 'small van taxi.'

In the table below, we provide examples of city varieties of three dialect groups and how they contrast with Putonghua (*Hanyu fangyin zihui*, 1989; *Hanyu fangyan gaiyao*, 1989). The pronunciation is provided in the International Phonetic Alphabet. Chinese characters indicate dialect similarities and differences in use:

Table 2

Sample Vocabulary from Selected City Dialects

Putonghua (Mandarin)	wo 我	ni 你	t'a 他，她	ʂl 石
Shanghai (Wu)	ŋu 我 aʔlaʔ	noŋ 儂	i 伊	zɒʔ 石
Xiamen (Southern Min or Hokkien)	gua 我	li 汝	i 伊	sɪk 石 tsioʔ
Guangzhou (Yue or Cantonese)	ŋɔ 我	nei 你	k'œy 佢	ʃɛk 石
	'I'	'you'	'he or she'	'stone'

Notice how the choice of Chinese characters for certain vocabulary differs. The character for the third person singular in Cantonese is one that is not used in standard Chinese. The two options for the first person singular in the Shanghai variety reflect two major geographic sources of migrants from the Wu dialect group area. The form, [ŋu], represents a westward origin from Suzhou and Wuxi. The form, [aʔlaʔ], represents a southward origin from Ningbo (*Hanyu fangyan gaiyao*, 1989). What further sociolinguistic meaning each of these forms possesses, we do not know.

The differences between the language varieties are not only issues of education, but the economy as well. The ability to code-switch between Putonghua and a major dialect is an asset to domestic business people in China today. The nature of code-switching and the degree to which it is necessary are topics that require further research. We can, however, provide an illustration of China's linguistic context by describing the speech community of Nanjing where our study takes place.

The Speech Community of Nanjing

Nanjing (pop. 6 million) is the only major metropolitan area in eastern China south of the Yangzi River that is Mandarin-speaking. The speech of its inhabitants is a part of the Southern Mandarin dialect group, but the city lies only fifty kilometers west of the line where the language varieties of the Wu dialect group begin. As an imperial capital for six dynasties and the capital of Republican China (1927-49), it is a city with a rich historical and cultural legacy. Consequently, it is home to a number of universities and institutes, and attracts many international students of the Chinese language. Second only to Beijing in numbers of international Chinese language students, its popularity stems from its history, its Mandarin-speaking population, and its access to South China.

Yet, the language spoken in Nanjing is not standard Putonghua, even though it is largely intelligible for people from Beijing. In the Nanjing dialect, many of the diphthongs in Putonghua are pronounced as monothongs. For example, *bái* 白 'white' becomes [be] or [bə]. In a bi-syllabic word, the diphthong [ai] becomes [ə] as in [bəttu] 白兔 'white rabbit.' Another example is the word *méiyǒu* 没有 'don't have.' In Nanjing the vowels in this word are pronounced as [mədə]. Also, there is the free variation between [n] and [l], evident throughout South China (DeFrancis, 1984). Some inhabitants pronounce the name of their city as [lantçiŋ]. There are borrowings from the Wu dialects: the tag question *duì bú duì* 对不对 'isn't it?' is expressed as [ara?].

Explanations for Nanjing's Northern speech, despite its southern location, are historical. Like the people from the areas around the Yellow River, Nanjing's inhabitants have been often on the move. Due more to politics than natural disasters, much of the population in the last 150 years has been replaced several times. In 1862, the defeat of the Taiping Rebellion almost completely destroyed the city. In 1937, Japanese troops terrorized the city in the infamous "Rape of Nanking" causing many of the inhabitants to flee. In 1949, the Nationalists abandoned their capital, taking with them many intellectuals and people with money. The bulk of the population was replaced not from the Wu-speaking Yangzi delta to the east, but from the areas of Anhui and Jiangsu Provinces to the north. However, the positions of leadership were not filled by these people, but rather by people from Shanghai and other parts of the delta. They included college presidents, factory managers, and high-level bureaucrats. Therefore the people in power, in addition to being speakers of Putonghua, were speakers of a Wu dialect. Indeed, students and friends alike have reported attempting to learn Wu, particularly Shanghainese, so that they too could have access to the discourse of power. Even newspaper articles admitted that Shanghainese was being studied by students ("Speaking in Tongues," 1991). We have witnessed this phenomenon for ourselves when we visited an office where the leadership was conducting an executive meeting, in Shanghainese, in the presence of staff who claimed to be Southern Mandarin monolinguals.

This diglossic situation is not a new one. Emily Honig (1992) describes the patterns of discrimination that Wu-speaking residents of Shanghai have inflicted on speakers of varieties of Southern Mandarin. These people, called sūbēirén 苏北 人 'people from Jiangsu Province north of the Yangzi River,' migrated to Shanghai often as refugees from floods, famine, and wars. Because of their poverty, they were prepared to perform jobs that were looked down on, such as pulling rickshaws and collecting garbage. To cope with such treatment, groups of people from specific areas banded together in native place associations. In Shanghai, as in other major industrial cities, native place associations played a vital role in providing migrating people with an identity and sources of finding employment (Perry, 1993). The role of dialects in developing this sense of solidarity cannot be underestimated.

More sociolinguistic research is needed to assess the position and functions of the major dialect groups today. Yet we are persuaded that in spite of the dissemination of Putonghua through education and the media, the dialects are not in retreat. And specifically, due to the economic status of the localities where the following are spoken, Wu (Shanghai), Southern Min (Xiamen/Taiwan), and Cantonese (Guangzhou/Hong Kong), these varieties appear to have become languages of prestige and power.

At the same time, speakers of Putonghua can be found nationwide. In Nanjing, as in every other locality in China, Putonghua is taught to all children in the first grade thereby creating a diglossic situation. There is a language variety for formal use and a variety for informal use. The teaching method too is uniform. The standard language is taught using a romanized alphabet. As children learn the alphabet, they learn the proper pronunciation of Putonghua. This method of using an alphabet is not an ancient practice to learn Chinese characters, but one that has been implemented only in this century.

The Development of an Alphabet for Chinese

Throughout its history, China has been in contact with people who neither spoke nor wrote Chinese. The Great Wall of China, although not a positive symbol of inter-ethnic communication, serves as a monument to the existence of contact between ethnic groups since ancient times. Contact with China, until the nineteenth century, almost inevitably involved a recognition of the superiority of its civilization. Consequently, the written language was learned by outsiders but rarely were literate Chinese motivated to acquire written languages of other peoples. The semantic nature of Chinese characters, as indicated earlier, allowed them to be used across unintelligible dialects. Even the foreign dynasties of the Liao, Jin, and Yuan, including the final dynasty, the Qing (1644-1911), founded by the Manchurians, used Chinese for their administration (Zhang Xiruo, 1955/1979). In the case of the Qing dynasty, official documents were written in both Chinese and Manchu (Fairbank, 1992). The Chinese language was essential because the written characters, *hànzì* 汉字, literally meaning the characters of the Han, served as a powerful cohesive force among the vast majority of the population who identified themselves as Chinese.

In the sixteenth century, when travelers from Europe began to arrive in steady numbers, a knowledge of Chinese was necessary for the success of their ventures, whether missionary or commercial. However, the Chinese language was not easily mastered, especially the written form. One of the first attempts to facilitate the language learning process for Europeans was made by Matteo Ricci (1552-1610), a Jesuit priest and missionary. He transcribed the sounds of Chinese using the Latin alphabet. He assumed that by giving Chinese the same familiar physical shapes as say Italian or English, Chinese could be successfully learned.

Through his close contacts with a number of scholars, Ricci was able to deal with the Chinese elite. Fluent in Chinese, he wrote books about western ideas such as astronomy for this select group and so became well known. In 1601 he was invited to Beijing, where four years later he published his romanized alphabet. Eager to convert this influential class of scholars, Ricci used the spoken language of the court officials as the model for his romanization (Norman, 1988; Serruys, 1962; Spence, 1984, 1992). After his death, Ricci's romanized alphabet was perfected by Nicholas Trigault, a French Jesuit working in Hangzhou. In the nineteenth century, other examples of romanized alphabets were developed, such as the Wade-Giles system and the system developed by the British Postal Service in Canton. The latter differed from previous ones because it was based on Cantonese as spoken in Guanzhou, rather than on the language of Beijing. One common characteristic of these early systems of romanization was the fact that they were developed by outsiders in order to learn how to pronounce Chinese characters. The need for an alphabet to replace Chinese characters was not felt internally because literacy remained largely the possession of officials, scholars, and the wealthy classes. Furthermore, people who were semiliterate were also able to use Chinese characters with varying success for different purposes.

Attitudes toward the notion of universal literacy began to change during the decline of the Qing dynasty. Paul Serruys (1962) describes a number of writing systems created by Chinese between 1892 and 1913. There were various reasons for this sudden burst of activity. Some reformers, for instance, were influenced by the work of Protestant missionaries who translated the Bible into local dialects. Other reformers were interested in language reform in order to promote education. This interest in providing greater access to education was partly a consequence of the increasing numbers of Chinese students studying in Japan. There they witnessed for themselves the effects of the Meiji government's educational reforms and the resulting widespread literacy. In the Chinese context, replacing Chinese characters by a new script was seen as one means of providing greater access to literacy. Another factor that prompted interest in language reform was the various military defeats inflicted on China, such as the Sino-Japanese War of 1894-95. These forced leading citizens to become concerned about China's modernization. In their efforts to strengthen the military and establish an industrial base, leaders began to consider ways of reforming the Chinese language (Zhou Enlai, 1958/1979; Zhou Youguang, 1986). The language reform movement, together with other social and political reform movements, was adopted as a strategy of national self-preservation.

The symbols used in the newly invented scripts were diverse. In 1892, Lu Zhuanzhang created one of the first alphabet systems designed by a Chinese (Hannas, 1997). His system used the Roman alphabet together with a few additional invented symbols. Another example of these new scripts was one invented in 1900 by Wang Zhao. He had studied in Japan and used the Japanese Kana syllabaries as a model for his script (Norman, 1988). The Kana syllabaries used symbols that were derived from parts of Chinese characters. Wang actively promoted his script in schools and thousands of books were published in it. Other scripts used arabic numerals, shorthand systems, or combinations such as Chinese character strokes with Roman letters.

Just as there was diversity in the kinds of symbols used in the scripts, there was also variation in the dialects that formed the base of the new scripts. Lu Zhuanzhang's alphabet was based on the Southern Min dialect, with additional symbols for transcribing other dialects. Chen Qiu, who invented a system using character stokes, based his system on the Wenzhou dialect, part of the larger Wu group (Serruys, 1962). Wang Zhao's script was based on Guanhua, the language of imperial government. From 1900 onwards, Guanhua became the dialect most commonly used for new scripts, thus enabling them to have wider access across the country.

The Qing reformers were well aware of the enormous gap between the spoken and written forms of Chinese. Written Chinese (wényán 文言) was very different from the modern spoken varieties. The differences included grammar but the main difference lay in the lexical structure. Words in Wenyan normally consisted of single Chinese characters, a shorthand compared to the two- and three-syllable compounds that are common in the spoken vernacular (Serruys, 1962). In Table 3, there is a saying from the Analects of Confucius (*Lunyu*, p. 103). The Wenyan form is compared with a modern rendition:

Table 3

Comparison of Wenyan and Modern Text

Wenyan	仁	者	必	有	勇		
	rén	zhě	bì	yǒu	yǒng		
Modern	仁	慈	的	人	必	有	勇 敢
	rén	cí	de	rén	bì	yǒu	yǒng gǎn

'The benevolent person will always be brave'

The modern spoken form, as can be seen above, contains more lexical items. There are more function words, and moreover, it reflects the tendency of spoken Chinese to have words consisting of more than one syllable (Huang & Liu, 1978).

The advantage of Wenyan, through the centuries, lay in its comprehensibility to readers who were speakers of various dialect groups, thus providing literary coherence throughout the empire. But since so few people were fully literate in Wenyan, such communication was often limited to only a small elite group. Yet, members of this group could be found in almost every locality within the empire. Moreover, there existed the unnumbered group of only partially literate people. This is why most Chinese people insist, in spite of the de facto multilingualism, that the Chinese language is one.

However, as the nineteenth century drew to a close, it became apparent to the reformers that unless there was a common spoken language and universal literacy, China would not be able to modernize. Although Wenyan served as a common written code, a spoken lingua franca was seen to be needed. The only realistic option was Guanhua, the language of the mandarins, based on the language used in Beijing. This variety did already serve as a kind of lingua franca (Zhou Youguang, 1986).

The Qing dynasty collapsed in 1911, but officials in the new republic were eager to continue language reform. They understood the utility of a common language to promote national unity. In 1913, a Conference on the Unification of Pronunciation was convened in Beijing and was composed of delegates from all over the country. The task of the conference focused on unifying the pronunciation of Chinese characters. Unfortunately, the selection of the Beijing dialect as a basis for the national standard caused resentment among the Southerners. It was therefore agreed that the new national standard would be a mixture of a number of dialects, even though the Beijing one dominated (Ramsey, 1987). Out of this conference, the Committee of the Unification of Pronunciation was formed. The Committee created a national phonetic alphabet to encode the pronunciation of the new national standard. This alphabet was called, *guóyīn zìmǔ* (kuoyin tzumu) 國音字母 (DeFrancis, 1984) or the National Phonetic Letters (Mathews, 1943). It was also called *zhùyīn fúhào* (chuyin fuhao) 注音符號. These letters did not resemble symbols of any Western alphabets. Instead, many of these symbols, like the Japanese Kana symbols, were derived from parts of Chinese characters. In Table 4 below are examples of selected symbols from the Guoyin Zimu alphabet:

Table 4

Comparison of Selected Guoyin Zimu Symbols with Hanyu Pinyin

Guoyin Zimu:	ㄚ	ㄧ	ㄙ	ㄑ
Hanyu Pinyin:	a	yi	s	q

Together with the publication of the Dictionary of National Pronunciation, *guóyīn zìdiǎn* (kuoyin tzudien) 國音字典, the new Ministry of Education began to focus on compiling textbooks and training teachers so that the national language could be taught in schools (*The Republic of China yearbook 1994*, 1993).

The new pronunciation system for the national language did not have popular appeal. Its weakness lay in being a mixture of regional dialects, and the Beijing dialect was not dominant enough to dispel the impression that the new language sounded artificial. In 1920 and 1921, a set of gramophone records was produced to help train teachers, but few succeeded in mastering this new standard (Ramsey, 1987). The movement for a common spoken language became crippled by heavy criticism. Furthermore, the political problems of the new republic, especially with the rise of the warlords and the resulting regionalism, did not help to promote such projects of national unity.

As a result, the Ministry of Education set about seeking a more viable national standard pronunciation. By 1924, Beijing pronunciation was agreed upon as the national standard (Zhou Youguang, 1986). This policy was confirmed by the 1932 publication of *guóyīn chángyòng zìhuì* (kuoyin ch'angyung tzihui) 國音常用字彙, a glossary of frequently used characters to represent the standard pronunciation (Mathews, 1943). The glossary was similar to an earlier one except that this new one was entirely based on the Beijing dialect, an existing vernacular. This reversal provoked little controversy, even though it implied that Guanhua, the language of the mandarins, was maintained and promoted just as the Qing reformers had advocated. The term *guóyǔ* (kuoyü) 國語 'national language,' already coined by the Japanese for their own language (Kokugo), was officially chosen as its new name.

The selection of a regional variety for a standard began a revolution in education. Zhou Youguang (1986) points out that instead of teaching reading using the local variety as a medium of instruction, beginning with the simplest Chinese characters and moving toward the complex ones, the sounds of the standard language had to be learned first. This was done by learning the Guoyin Zimu alphabet. After the alphabet was mastered, then Chinese characters were learned based on Beijing pronunciation. The aim was to spread this method to all children in elementary school, beginning in grade one. In the 1930s, the nationalist government vigorously promoted the use of Guoyu and Guoyin Zimu in the schools.

This method of using an alphabet to teach the sounds of the standard language before learning Chinese characters continues today both on the mainland and in Taiwan. However, the use of Guoyin Zimu continues only in Taiwan (*The Republic of China yearbook 1994,* 1993). Through our own contacts with educators in Taiwan, we have found that support is still strong for the use of Guoyin Zimu, because unlike Roman letters, it is claimed the symbols of this system do not become a source of interference when Chinese speakers learn a European language. The same problem of interference is avoided when the Chinese language is learned as a foreign language.

Not all reformers supported the selection of Beijing Chinese as a base for a national standard language. Communist Party member Qu Qiubai, for example, asserted that Guoyu represented the language of the Qing court; therefore, the historical connection cast the choice as elitist. He urged the use of what he called Putonghua, the common language of the people, to unite the speech of China. The problem with Qu's assertion lay in his broad definition of Putonghua. The language was supposed to be based on the real speech of the urban proletariat, but the question remained, which group of urban proletarians? After the Communists came to power in 1949, Qu Qiubai's own term, "Putonghua" was adopted as the name for the standard language (DeFrancis, 1984), even though, as mentioned earlier, the Putonghua of the Communist government turned out to be almost identical to the existing Guoyu. Yet changing the name suggests an attempt to preserve Qu's vision of a common language devoid of age-old elitisms. While the language itself remained unchanged, the phonemic representation of Putonghua took a different course than that of Guoyu.

In addition to Wenyan and Guanhua, the reformers possessed another resource. There existed a popular genre of literature that was based on the narrative prose of storytellers (Rawski, 1979) and the more informal uses of written language found in plays, songs, and personal letters (Serruys, 1962). Since the mid-nineteenth century, missionaries produced literature written with local speech patterns and soon vernacular newspapers were being published in many cities around 1900 (Link, 1981). One linguistic explanation for the difference between Wenyan and the textual styles based on speech lay in the difference in morphology. In Wenyan, words tend to be represented by single syllables. In speech, words tend to be two or more syllables long.

This "vernacular" style, called *báihuà* 白话, was to be widely identified with the May Fourth Movement. The movement began in 1919 as a student-led protest against the Treaty of Versailles that granted to Japan Germany's treaty ports in China. The protest went further in calling for reforms in China's politics and society. The use of Baihua became one of the rallying points. What is significant in the aftermath of the May Fourth Movement is that Baihua became respectable since many intellectuals accepted the notion of literature based on actual speech patterns (Link, 1981). As a result, a serious rival to Wenyan was created. Although Baihua was heavily influenced by speech (Norman, 1988), it quickly evolved into a literary genre with its own characteristics.

Most reformers agreed that Baihua, rather than Wenyan, should guide the standard written language. However, some reformers, including Qu Qiubai, felt that even Baihua was too elitist. He was especially critical of the writings of the May Fourth Movement which he felt were too foreign and incomprehensible to the general public (Link, 1981). He also questioned the very use of Chinese characters. In their stead, Qu urged the adoption of a completely different writing system, *lādīnghuà xīn wénzì* (Latinxua Sin Wenz) 拉丁化新文字 'Latinization New Writing.' Working with Chinese and Russian colleagues in the Soviet Union during the late 1920s, Qu Qiubai had developed a writing system for Chinese immigrants living in Russia. Using the Roman alphabet, Ladinghua Xin Wenzi was based on the language spoken in Northern China, specifically Shangdong province. Although the system did not contain any tone markers, it was considered successful in promoting literacy. Qu later brought it to China where it was used to develop literacy based on local dialects in a number of regions. Even though his efforts were criticized as promoting regionalism, Qu received support for the use of Ladinghua Xin Wenzi from prominent intellectuals, such as author Lu Xun and also the Communist party. Paul Serruys (1962) further points out that during the years at Yanan, the Communist base during the Anti-Japanese War (1937-1945), the Communist party used this romanized alphabet to develop materials for its literacy program.

Ladinghua Xin Wenzi was not the only romanized writing system in the Republican period. In 1923, the Chinese Romanization Spelling Research Committee, a scholarly body, developed its own system of romanization. By 1926, the committee had produced the Guoyeu Romatzyh Spelling System (*guóyǔ luómǎzì* 國語羅馬字), based on the Beijing dialect (DeFrancis, 1984). This system differed from Ladinghua Xin Wenzi primarily by tone representation. Tone was not indicated by diacritics as in Hanyu Pinyin, but by insertions of certain letters that would indicate the tone (Norman, 1988). In Table 5, the transcription of syllables with Guoyeu Romatzyh is contrasted with Hanyu Pinyin.

Table 5

Comparison of Guoyeu Romatzyh with Hanyu Pinyin

Standard Tones	1	2	3	4
Guoyeu Romatzyh	wen	wern	ween	wenn
Hanyu Pinyin	wēn	wén	wěn	wèn
汉字	温	文	稳	问
	'warm'	'text'	'stability'	'question'

Although Guoyeu Romatzyh was adopted as an official romanization in 1928 by the Ministry of Education, it did not gain wide appeal and was only adopted in a few dictionaries (Serruys, 1962; DeFrancis, 1984). The popular *Mathews' Chinese-English dictionary* (1943), for example, mentions the system in its introduction but does not use it in the entries. The idea of representing tone through the letters themselves is an attractive one, since tone in Chinese is phonemic and the representation through letters would offer the reader finer distinctions. The system might have possessed a visual advantage over Hanyu Pinyin, because even with the tone diacritics over Hanyu Pinyin syllables, visually, the syllables look like homonyms. In spite of the possible advantages of Guoyeu Romatzyh, political developments led to its virtual abandonment.

In 1949, the Nationalist government fled to Taiwan and the Communist Party came to power. Like those who gained control in 1911, the Communists in 1949 faced enormous challenges to unite and modernize China. The years of the Anti-Japanese War (1937-45) and the Civil War (1946-49) had destroyed much of the economy. Moreover, the years of war emphasized divisions between people, in spite of a common enemy. As a part of the unifying process, the problems of illiteracy needed to be addressed, not only among the multilingual Han Chinese, but also among the many ethnic minorities. The solution was to require everyone to learn standard Chinese. In 1949, the Association for Reforming the Chinese Written Language was established and it immediately began working on issues of language reform (Wu Yuzhang, 1958).

However, the Communists varied in their approach to language reform.

There were those influenced by Qu Qiubai, such as Wu Yuzhang, who had used the romanized script, Ladinhua Xin Wenzi, in literacy campaigns. They did not want to simplify the Chinese characters since they assumed that these would eventually be replaced by a phonetic script. In a 1951 speech, Mao Zedong said: "The written language must be reformed; we must proceed in the direction of phoneticization being taken by all languages of the world" (Wen, 1973/1979, p. 349). This was not to be interpreted as the replacement of Chinese characters by a phonetic script. In spite of the efficiency in spreading literacy by means of an alphabet, there was stiff resistance to its use. Support was stronger, instead, for simplified Chinese characters. In addition to the sway of traditionalist and indigenous sentiments, this propensity for maintaining Chinese characters, even in simplified form, is perhaps further evidence for the prevalence of partial literacy. The struggle over the nature of the language reforms was reflected in further name changes for the association. In 1952, it became the Research Committee for Reforming the Chinese Written Language. Then in 1954, it was reorganized and became the Committee for Reform of the Chinese Written Language, with the reforms focusing, according to Wu Yuzhang (1958), on the following areas:

> (a) the simplification of Chinese characters so that illiteracy could be eliminated;
> (b) the use of a common national language, Putonghua, to foster national unity;
> (c) the development of a phonetic alphabet to help promote Putonghua.

The work was to be done in stages, often simultaneously, beginning with simplifying the Chinese characters and evolving a phonetic spelling system to promote a standard language. Eventually these reforms would culminate in a phoneticization of the Chinese script which would enable more people to become literate. Chinese characters could be reformed, but they were not to be abolished. The committee, composed of people from various backgrounds including scholars and cadres, invited suggestions and comments from the public. These reforms were intended to be a reflection of the will of the people, in line with the government's political philosophy of involving the masses. Although this democratic aspect of the language reform process may have been new, the desire to reform the Chinese language was not; the Communists were only continuing a tradition that had begun thousands of years earlier when the first Qin emperor had reformed the writing system.

Language Reforms

The Simplification of Characters

The Committee for Reform of the Chinese Written Language collected examples of simplified characters as well as produced their own, and by January 1955, three lists of simplified characters were drafted. These were circulated and finally promulgated by the State Council in January 1956. The initial stage of simplification had three parts, the first consisting of a list of 230 simplified characters. The second list consisted of a further 285 simplified characters. Of these, 95 characters were classified as experimental. The third list was composed of 54 simplified radicals. Of the total, 355 simplified characters were immediately used in newspapers and school textbooks. The first list was generally widely accepted since the majority of the reforms reflected informal usage; however, the second and third lists had to be revised (Zhou Youguang, 1986).

There were two main methods of simplifying characters: reducing the overall number of characters and reducing the number of strokes per character. With each, the committee used a variety of different approaches. For instance, when reducing the number of characters, the committee could select one character to represent homophones written with different characters (Chan & He, 1988).

Simplification by reducing the number of strokes per character was a complicated process and involved various procedures. For instance, parts of a character could be deleted or simpler components could replace more complex ones. In general, the simplification process produced more difficulties for readers since it became increasingly difficult to distinguish between characters. They were perhaps easier to write but not to read (Coulmas, 1989; Hannas, 1997; Xie, 1989). In Table 6, selected methods of character simplification are illustrated.

32

Table 6

Selected Methods of Chinese Character Simplification

General reduction of strokes:

龜 —> 龟
guī   guī
'tortoise'

Selection of parts of characters:

豐 —> 丰
fēng   fēng
'bountiful'

Simplification of radicals:

言 —> 讠
yán   yán
'speech'

Replacement with simpler components:

範 —> 范
fàn   fàn
'specificity'

Calligraphic cursive forms:

門 —> 门
mén   mén
'gate'

Merging homophones and near homophones:

捲 + 卷 —> 卷
juǎn   juǎn   juǎn and juǎn
'roll up'   'volume'   'roll up and volume'

Each of the above approaches to simplification is not necessarily mutually exclusive. Many of the simplified radicals were also based on age-old calligraphic cursive forms. Although China's character simplification efforts have been criticized from the standpoint of losing their comprehensibility with other languages that use Chinese characters like Korean and Japanese, we have observed that Japanese people, literate in calligraphic cursive forms, can decode many of the simplified characters in the People's Republic of China.

As the simplified characters were integrated into the written language, a total of 2,238 simplified characters emerged from the original 2264 complex ones. These characters varied in the average number of strokes per character, but in general, they had from 8 to 11 strokes when compared with the originals that had, on average, from 16 to 19 strokes (Chan & He, 1988). By using a variety of approaches to simplification, the committee had produced characters that reflected current informal and calligraphic usage as well as completely new experimental ones. A General List of all these simplified characters, including revisions from the earlier 1956 lists, was published in 1964.

In December 1977, after the fall of the Gang of Four and a return to stability, a new list of simplified characters was published. This was known as the Second Scheme for the Simplification of Characters and consisted of 853 simplified characters as well as 61 simplified components of characters. The press immediately began to use some of the new forms but within six months, these characters were all withdrawn because of the fierce opposition to them. Critics claimed that the simplification process had gone too far and that many of the new characters were confusing or even too alien. Unlike the reforms of 1956, these proposals had not been widely circulated beforehand nor did they reflect informal current usage (C. Cheng, 1985; Zhou Youguang, 1986). The reformers' experiments with character simplification had gone beyond popular usage. Those who were already literate or partially literate would have to learn again how to read and this was untenable.

In 1980, the Committee for Reform of the Chinese Written Language was reorganized and set about revising the abortive 1977 list. It soon produced a revised list of 111 simplified characters, but these were also withdrawn as the Committee felt that this revision lacked sufficient political support to obtain approval by the State Council (Rohsenow, 1986). In 1985, the committee was yet again renamed and reorganized, this time being called the National Committee on Language and Script Work. One of its first tasks was formally to withdraw the controversial 1977 list of simplified characters. In 1986, it produced a slightly revised version of the 1964 General List, but no further reforms of the written language have since been published.

C. Cheng (1985) points out that one of the main reasons for the failure of the 1977 and 1980 proposals was the rapidity of all the language reforms, especially since the new simplified characters would undermine what had already been learned in school. "It is rather disconcerting to find that what was learned a few years ago has to be relearned" (C. Cheng, 1985, p. 6). Taking 10 to 12 years as an average for years of schooling, he suggests that there should be a minimum of 20 to 24 years, that is, double the number of years of schooling, before changes are introduced. The longer the period between the implementation of further language changes, the more likely that they would succeed since these reforms would not be seen as eroding a person's hard won literacy. Perhaps this is the case in China today, as no further changes in character simplification have been introduced since 1986.

Since the 1970s and the opening up of the Chinese economy, the use of the older, complex characters in advertisements and notices has increased. Unlike the simplified characters, the older characters are still regarded as more prestigious (He, 1993; Su, 1991). The government has tried to crack down on the illegal use of the older forms. For instance, during the 1991 Asian Games, officials in Beijing went round the city removing notices with the older-style characters (Kohut, 1991), but the practice continues.

A National Language

Like the previous Nationalist government, the Communists regarded fostering a national identity by means of a common language as a more urgent task than accounting for regional varieties. This was reflected in Wu Yuzhang's address to the First National People's Congress in 1958: "They stand in urgent need of a common language, the lack of which causes certain inconveniences in the political, economic, and cultural life of the Chinese people" (Wu Yuzhang, 1958, p. 38). An article by Stalin, published in 1950, on the need to promote the use of Russian as a national language, was used to support the propagation of Putonghua (DeFrancis, 1984). However, Putonghua was not intended to replace local dialects. Instead, Putonghua and local speech varieties were to have clearly defined functions, with the overall intention of fostering national unity and the ability to communicate at a national level. This was emphasized by Wu in his address to the 1958 Congress.

> Dialects are also useful media of social intercourse. They serve the
> people of specific regions. But their use is confined to the regions

concerned. Outside of this limit, they are of no use as media of social intercourse and become an impediment to mutual understanding. (p. 39-40)

At the same time, Wu made it clear that while everyone needed to use Putonghua, varying standards of fluency were acceptable. Those in the media and education were expected to speak Putonghua fluently and accurately. However, "no strict demands should be made on the common people" (1958, p. 41). What counted was making the effort to learn and use Putonghua and this commitment to a political ideal was more important than linguistic accuracy. The policy was not easy to implement, especially in non-Mandarin speaking rural areas. Glen Peterson (1994) describes how Party officials in Guangdong Province focused on village leaders rather than on all the villagers, making the ability to speak Putonghua a criterion for leadership. Thus linguistic skill in Putonghua became a means of social mobility and professional advancement.

The 1956 reforms stated that the primary reason for learning Putonghua was to promote national unity by means of a standard language. That goal remains (Gong, 1994). The state has recognized the importance of bilingual education for certain minority groups, whereby the local language is learned in addition to Putonghua and Chinese characters (X. Li, 1992; "United in Speaking 53 Languages," 1991). In practice, however, a lack of funding, materials, and teachers, as well as the belief that a knowledge of Putonghua and Chinese characters is more advantageous, have undermined bilingual education (Lin, 1997; Yin & Baldauf, 1990). Putonghua is vigorously promoted as the language for national unity as illustrated by a 1996 beauty contest in Hong Kong. One of the criteria was being able to read aloud a Chinese character text in fluent Putonghua rather than in Cantonese, the main language of Hong Kong. This caused difficulty and embarrassment for many of the contestants (Clemetson, 1996).

The Development of Hanyu Pinyin

In 1952, the Research Committee for Reforming the Chinese Written Language was established to work on language reform. After two years, it was reorganized, with a new sub-committee to work on the phonetic alphabet. Wu Yuzhang, director of the main committee for language reform, maintained that six different systems for a phonetic alphabet were presented for discussion at a national conference on language reform. These included one based on Cyrillic as well as one using the Latin alphabet. In February 1956, the Draft Scheme for a Chinese Phonetic Alphabet was published. The new alphabetic system, Hanyu Pinyin, was designed to be used only as a teaching tool for the learning of Putonghua. Hanyu Pinyin, based on the Latin alphabet, had a maximum of four letters per syllable. Unlike the earlier Ladinghua Xin Wenzi, Hanyu Pinyin used tone marks in dictionary entries, except for foreign words or unaccentuated syllables (Serruys, 1962). The intention was not to replace Chinese characters with Hanyu Pinyin. Instead, it was to function as a romanized spelling system for educational and documentation purposes. Between 1957 and 1962, a number of lists were published to standardize, in Putonghua, words that had multiple readings. Although this project was interrupted for many years, it was resumed in 1982. Zhou Youguang (1986) emphasizes the continuing importance of this project, especially in the light of new ideas in science and technology and the increase of loan words.

No sooner was the draft published than plans were made for primary and secondary teachers to be trained in Putonghua and Hanyu Pinyin so that they could function as models for the children in school. In 1958, the Ministry of Education directed all school children to learn Hanyu Pinyin. Already by 1959, officials were praising the success of the program (Wei, 1959/1979; Wu Yuzhang, 1959/1979).

These reforms were controversial. Perhaps anticipating criticism, the committee published numerous books and articles describing the historical precedents of the language reforms. These included dictionaries and various scripts, especially alphabet systems, invented over the years (Serruys, 1962). Even so, regarding the use of Hanyu Pinyin, one critic, Tang Lan (1957/1979) claimed that it would be more efficient to introduce a number of phonetic Chinese characters. This approach, he maintained, would be preferable to using an alien writing system. To implement this system, he "would gradually develop a phonetic system of writing on the original base of the Chinese characters, using their inherent forms" (p. 97). A romanized alphabet would be too time-consuming and impractical to implement, especially since the goals of the reform were to promote unity and literacy.

The 'phonetic spelling of Chinese' . . . requires that we first complete the work of spreading the use of the standard vernacular (putonghua) and of standardizing the Chinese language, which is not something that can be done quickly. . . . Even after the standard verncaular is in widespread use and the Chinese language has been made to agree with the model, creating an entirely new system of writing still will not be an easy matter. (p. 98)

Others were also opposed to the use of a Roman alphabet because they felt it was "un-Chinese." Xu Mumin (1957/1979) argued passionately against romanization:

The Latin alphabet is not our national product; it is a stranger to the people in general in our country. As Chairman Mao has said, we have our national forms. We should use our national form of writing. . . . If we do Latinize Chinese writing, then we will be fighting the world for Latin writing! If we do, we will not be able to face our ancestors and we will not be able to face our descendants; our ancestors will berate us for not being 'sons who bring honor to the family' and our descendants will berate us for having surrendered our teachers! (p. 200)

Opposition to the new alphabet did not die; in fact, it became more vocal with the brief liberalization known as the "100 Flowers Movement." In Guangdong Province, opposition to using Hanyu Pinyin had a different twist. Party officials endorsed the use of separate alphabetical schemes based on the Province's four main dialects, rather than use the standard Putonghua-based Hanyu Pinyin alphabet. They claimed that it would be easier to promote literacy in the rural areas via local dialects, rather than impose a double burden of the strange phonetic script and strange official language of Putonghua (Peterson, 1994). Although this project soon failed, it does indicate that the official policy from Beijing was not easily implemented.

In spite of these sentiments, the authorities promoted romanization. Hanyu Pinyin was revised before being finally presented, in November 1957, to the State

Council where the romanization system was accepted. The National People's Congress ratified this decision in early 1958.

In a key speech on language reform made to the National Political Consultative Conference in 1958, Premier Zhou Enlai summarized the argument for the adoption of a romanized alphabet as the basis for teaching the common language. The Beijing dialect was to continue to be used as the basis of standard Chinese, as this choice was considered essential for the promotion of national unity. Hanyu Pinyin had been developed to ensure the standard pronunciation of Putonghua. To those who feared that the use of Hanyu Pinyin threatened the existence of Chinese characters, Zhou Enlai (1958/1979) assured them with the following remarks:

> At the outset, we should make clear that the purpose of the 'Plan for the Phonetic Spelling of Chinese' is to indicate the pronunciation of Chinese characters and to spread the use of the standard vernacular; it is not to substitute a phonetic writing system for the Chinese characters. (p. 235)

In the same spirit, Zhou Enlai asserted that the learning of a standard language was not intended to replace the dialects, but rather to facilitate communication between people. In his speech, Zhou Enlai stressed that Hanyu Pinyin "will be extremely beneficial in teaching reading in primary schools and in sweeping away illiteracy" (p. 236). Although a Roman alphabet was to be adopted, it was not to be the Guoyin Zimu nor the Ladinghua Xin Wenzi systems. These earlier systems, Zhou Enlai claimed, were more difficult, but the new romanized alphabet would be easier to learn and remember. He further listed other reasons for endorsing the use of Hanyu Pinyin: it would make it easier for the different minority groups to learn Chinese, thus promoting national unity, and it would help foreigners learn Chinese and so foster mutual understanding and cooperation. Zhou Enlai's speech was intended to quell any further opposition to the language reforms. It is still regarded today as a crucial document indicating the purpose and direction of language reform in the People's Republic of China.

These decisions, made in the mid-1950s, continue to be in force. The turmoil of the Cultural Revolution and the resulting disruption of education have not changed the way children become literate in the schools. Hanyu Pinyin continues to serve as the link between the spoken Putonghua and the written Chinese characters. The revised Constitution of 1982 stressed the importance of Putonghua, and therefore the role of Hanyu Pinyin as the means to teach standard pronunciation.

Despite the introduction of simplified characters, difficulties still exist in their acquisition and use. From the outset of the language reform process, the committee made it clear that simplification of characters would not fully eliminate the problems of becoming literate. Chinese characters are not a phonetic system and are thus not easy to use. There has been no word of any plans to develop a phonetic script to replace the characters and Hanyu Pinyin remains only a spelling system, not a writing system. The language reform movement has only proceeded to the initial stages of the process as outlined in the early 1950s, that is, simplifying characters and developing a phonetic spelling system to teach the characters. Even these steps are indicative of a monumental task that has already been achieved.

Summary

The unity of the Chinese language in the midst of its diversity is based on three elements: a. Chinese characters, b. Wenyan (the classical written language) and c. Guanhua (the speech of the mandarins). These three elements are listed in the order of salience in promoting the sense of linguistic unity. Chinese characters, used throughout the Chinese empire as well as in Japan and Korea, have proved to be adaptable to various phonemic systems. Their ubiquitous presence in the visual arts, for instance in calligraphy on paintings, has reinforced their prominence in Chinese civilization.

Readers and writers of Wenyan, classical Chinese, existed in all regions that adopted Chinese characters, including Japan. But these literate people made up only a small proportion of the population. Few had access to enough education to become literate in Wenyan. The strength of Chinese characters as a unifying factor lay in the possibility that many Chinese people possessed varying degrees of literacy skills which they believed adequate for their purposes. In other words, they believed they had sufficient return on their investment. Perhaps some frequently used characters were comprehended by a vastly larger population than is normally estimated.

The weakest of the three elements of linguistic unity, Guanhua, functioned as a lingua franca throughout the empire. Still, it served as the grandparent to modern Putonghua, which like its parent Guoyu, was modeled closely after the Guanhua spoken in and around Beijing. Significant numbers of reformers both in the revolutions of 1911 and 1949 called for a standard language of China that would be more inclusive of its linguistic diversity. In both cases, the result was a triumph for the cultural conservatives: the Guanhua tradition was continued. Yet, the names adopted for the language bear witness to the ideals of each revolution. Guoyu is the language of the nation (i.e., the language of the Nationalists). Putonghua is the common language of the people (i.e., the language of the people's party, the Communists).

The selection of a standard language, accordingly, required a serious attempt to reach universal literacy. To do so, alphabets were developed in order to facilitate teaching the standard speech first and then Chinese characters. For Guoyu, the non-Roman Guoyin Zimu alphabet was adopted. For Putonghua, the Roman Hanyu Pinyin alphabet was adopted. The Sino-centric Guoyin Zimu alphabet fitted well with the Nationalist view of Chinese nationhood. The Hanyu Pinyin of the Communist regime fitted well with an ideology that was potentially universal, despite the isolationism of the regime itself. Hanyu Pinyin, as a Roman alphabet, provided the potential for connection, if not a universal one, with the majority of the rest of the people in the world.

The adoption of an alphabet to aid literacy did not fulfill the dream of reformers such as Qu Qiubai for an alphabet to replace Chinese characters. To be literate in Chinese today, the ability to read and write Chinese characters is required. Knowledge of only Hanyu Pinyin is inadequate. Hanyu Pinyin is only a caretaker script. However, a selective knowledge of only a small number of Chinese characters might be functionally adequate.

Instead of replacing Chinese characters with Hanyu Pinyin, the main effort of script reform has been the simplification of Chinese characters. Although several stages of simplification have been achieved, it appears that any further changes are unlikely because of the strong opposition they would encounter. In fact with the liberalization of the economy, the older, complex characters are enjoying a revival, despite official opposition to their use.

Access to literacy in Chinese characters, however, has been restricted to, or rather channeled through, the standard spoken language of Putonghua. In the schools, children must first learn how to speak Putonghua. Although the Hanyu Pinyin alphabet serves as a bridge from Putonghua to written text in Chinese characters, the fact that this procedure is followed in the schools ensures that the standard spoken language is indeed taught across the nation. In the chapters that follow, the process of learning to read and write using this procedure is described in detail. In chapter two, we describe the contemporary social context in which children learn to read. We focus primarily on the institutional contexts, specifically the schools.

Chapter Two
The Schools

The process of learning to read cannot be reduced to a description of only a few words. Reading, like most forms of human behavior, is a complex network of interrelated factors. The first difficulty in describing the process of learning to read is pinpointing where the process actually begins. Studies in recent years, particularly those with an ethnographic orientation, have documented the existence of preschool literacy acquisition in the home, and these studies describe how such learning relates to learning at school (e.g., Heath, 1983; Leseman & de Jong, 1998; Morrow, Tracy, & Maxwell, 1995). Activities such as coaching the child in speaking or reading are well-known among parents as techniques to provide children with emergent literacy (Ollila & Mayfield, 1992). Indeed, most children come to school already exposed to the world of scripts and how these scripts represent speech and real-world meaning. In our study, we have documented examples of children who come to kindergarten already being able to read. Their ability is not limited to the Hanyu Pinyin alphabet, but includes Chinese characters. One five-year-old boy at Nanjing University Kindergarten was able to read his classmates' names in Chinese characters and so was able to help the teacher pass out workbooks.

While the home may provide an effective environment for learning, schools also play a significant role in children's learning. It is in school that the children's differing abilities and degrees of literacy background converge. Here the children compete, and are assessed and compared with each other. Moreover, it is the children's skills in literacy that provide a basis for classroom success. In our study, we describe the initial literacy acquisition process in school. Although we cannot ignore factors at home, and indeed we have been informed by the teachers that the successful children tend to be the ones who receive support at home, it is in the school where the child's language ability is launched in a real-world setting. It is through the dynamics of the classroom that many children learn the social meanings ascribed to speaking well, writing well, and reading well.

Elementary schools in China are not entirely a product of the twentieth century. In traditional Chinese society, there were schools available for children, even for those who were not being prepared for the civil service examinations. These schools, particularly during the rule of the Qing dynasty (1644-1911), included village, community, clan, and charitable types of schools. Although the level of opportunity to attend varied according to locality, schools did exist all over the empire. Evelyn Rawski (1979) points out that having an educated person in the family was seen to be a key to prosperity. It is estimated that in the latter half of the nineteenth century, 30 to 45% of Chinese men and 2 to 10% of Chinese women possessed functional literacy skills and this was largely the result of the schools (Rawski, 1979, p. 140).

In this study, we focus on urban elementary schools in the 1990s. We describe the classroom learning environment in two types of Chinese urban schools. One is a well-funded experimental school and the other is a local neighborhood school. The experimental school draws pupils from the entire city, while the other school draws pupils from a specific neighborhood. Both are relatively well-equipped. In both schools the number of children in each class is 55 or over, well above the recommended number. The large classes indicate demand and thus the good reputation of the schools.

For us to gain entry to these schools was not an easy task. The difficulty lay in the fact that we were not asking for a single school visit, but long-term classroom observation. Yet, in spite of initial resistance, probably due to the possible difficulties we might cause to those involved, entry to both schools was granted. However, the manner in which we were able to gain entry differed for both schools.

The Key School

On September 5, 1990, after a year of inquiry and careful negotiations, we finally obtained entry to a school. On that day, together with Zhu Jialong of the Teaching Research Institute of the Jiangsu Province Educational Commission (江苏省教育委员会教研室), we arrived at the school gate. We walked through the gate onto a broad driveway. To the left, stood a new three-story building with multi-colored tiles. The playground equipment was freshly painted. This was the kindergarten attached to the school.

Just beyond the kindergarten was a large track field and behind it loomed a five-story classroom building. The six classrooms on each floor opened onto a balcony that spanned the length of the building. In the center of the building was a stairway. There were also stairways at both ends of the building. On each floor, near the central stairway, was a single framed portrait. The portraits included Mao Zedong, Zhou Enlai, Lenin, and Lei Feng (雷锋)—the selfless army hero wearing a furry cap with loose ear flaps. To the left of the track field stood a large square building with brown tiles. We were proudly informed that this building housed the new indoor swimming pool. "Yes," Mr. Zhu remarked, "the facilities are good here at Changjiang Road School."

The principal of the school, Ms. Qian, met us at the door to her office and invited us in. After seating us and having the secretary serve us tea in capped porcelain mugs, she proceeded to give us an introduction to the school. Although the present buildings were new, the school was always a well-equipped one. It was founded by Christian missionaries in 1939. The principal did not know whether the original name of the school, Leisi Xuexiao (Leiszu Hsüehsiao) 類思學校, referred to the name of the missionary founder or meant literally 'school of various thoughts.' In 1946, the school was renamed Xinsheng Xiaoxue (Hsinsheng Hsiaohsüeh) 新生小學 'new life elementary school' in honor of the New Life Movement, a social renewal program launched by the Nationalist government in the 1930s. Xinsheng Xiaoxue remained a private elementary school until 1952 when the Nanjing city government took control of the school. The name was changed again in 1954 to its present one, which simply refers to its address.

Changjiang Road School 长江路小学 is designated a key school, and therefore serves as an experimental site for new teaching materials and methodologies. Key schools in urban areas tend to have a history of academic excellence that predates the Liberation of 1949 (Peterson, 1994). Changjiang Road School provides an accelerated program compressing the six years of elementary school into five. (In 1995, due to overcrowding in the middle schools, the program was expanded to six years). There are 1050 pupils, of whom 536 are boys and 414 are girls. There are four classes in every grade and a total of 20 classes covering the five years of elementary education. Altogether the school has 52 teachers and administrative staff. These include 3 teachers for physical education, 2 for art, 2 for music, 2 for nature and geography, 2 for English, 20 for math and 20 for *yŭwén* 语文 'Chinese language.' The math teachers assist in teaching other subjects while the Yuwen teachers serve as homeroom teachers and are also responsible for teaching ethics.

While the school offers demonstration classes for teachers in other Nanjing schools to come and observe, the school has no teacher-training college attached, unlike other inservice training centers. During our period of observation, we, on occasion, ran into faculty members from the largest teacher-training institution in the province, Nanjing Normal University. One time we met a teacher from Urumchi, the capital of Xinjiang Autonomous Region bordering Khazakstan, receiving inservice training. She was, however, an exception as we discovered that the school was designated to serve teachers of schools within the city of Nanjing.

To help facilitate the demanding accelerated program as well as the inservice teacher-training program, the school hired Ms. Wang Lan, a retired model teacher as a consultant on teaching Putonghua and Hanyu Pinyin. Wang Lan had formerly worked as a full-time teacher at Changjiang Road School, joining the teaching staff in 1955. As a consultant, she does not teach classes herself, but instead observes the teachers in the school and periodically conducts workshops for teachers from other schools. During the weeks we were allowed to observe the Yuwen classes, Wang Lan often interrupted the class to offer advice to the teacher. This kind of on the spot advisement was provided in lieu of a consultation after class.

We assumed that admittance to such a well-equipped, well-staffed school must depend on a rigorous entrance examination. Our assumptions were mistaken. Wang Lan bluntly explained that children were admitted to Changjiang Road School based on *guānxī* 关系 'connections.' The school offers a set number of places to the major public offices, companies, and factories in the city, and the leaders of these work units pass out the slots as perks to their promising young employees. As a result, the Yuwen teachers at Changjiang Road School had to cope with a fairly wide range of literacy skills and reading readiness.

Studies have been carried out describing the sociology of guanxi and how it relates to education (e.g., Delany & Paine, 1991; Kipnis, 1996). The horizontal exchange of gifts, favors, and influence is vital for most ventures large and small. Guanxi is described metaphorically in amounts. One can have lots of it or not enough of it to get something done. The fact that we gained entry to two schools and a kindergarten suggests that we possessed a sufficient amount of guanxi to achieve our goals.

The Neighborhood School

In September 1993, we were met by a well-dressed woman in her mid-30s at the gate of Yizhongxin School where without any formalities we were escorted directly to a classroom. Wang Mei, who had been made a model teacher, allowed us to observe her class for the six weeks of Putonghua and Hanyu Pinyin instruction. We had little difficulty gaining entry to this school. A few years earlier, Ms. Wang had taught two American girls in her class. Although they had ceased to attend Yizhongxin School, their mother maintained a relationship with Wang Mei and provided the introduction. Over dinner in June we made arrangements for the observations in the following fall. When the class was ready to start on September 5, Wang Mei contacted us by telephone and the next morning we rode our bicycles over to the school.

Wang Mei led us through a broad driveway lined with gingko trees. On the right was a row of glassed-in bulletin boards containing thematic displays and pictures of pupils with distinction. On the other side was a flower garden with red and golden cockscomb bushes in full bloom. There were two new buildings in the school that already tightly accommodated 1100 students. The smaller four-story building contained administrative offices. The larger four-story building, similar to the classroom building at Changjiang Road School, had balconies serving as hallways between classrooms. There were also portraits on each floor of the school as well. However, at this school a greater variety of exemplary persons was displayed including Confucius, Isaac Newton, and Marie Curie, as well as the usual Mao Zedong, Zhou Enlai, and Lei Feng.

The school was established in 1933 by a private individual. Neither Wang Mei nor the vice principal was able to identify who this founder was, but the private school that resulted was called Wutaishan Xiaoxue (Wutaishan Hsiaohsüeh) 五台山小學, named after the nearby hill. Regarding schools of this kind, Evelyn Rawski (1979, pp. 157-158) comments, "with the exception of missionary efforts, early attempts to create modern elementary schools were confined to private citizens." Although the city took over the school in the 1950s, the school retained its name until the city reorganized the schools in the early 1980s. Now the school is called Yizhongxin Xiaoxue 一中心小学 'First Central School,' a name that also refers to its location near the center of Nanjing.

Although the school is also located near Nanjing University, it has few pupils who are children of faculty and staff. This is because university housing lies in another school district. Wang Mei claims that about half of the children come from homes of intellectuals—that is, a family with a parent who has received some kind of tertiary education—while the other half consists of families of workers and owners of *gètǐhù* 个体户 'small private businesses.' Up until the late 1980s, pupils in neighborhood schools tended to come from the same background, as the schools would draw children from clearly defined neighborhoods. In the past, jobs were assigned and most jobs were administered by a *dānwèi* 单位 'work unit,' be it an office, factory, hospital, or school. The danwei provided housing and education. Today, people have greater freedom to select their own places of employment, and consequently, neighborhoods are becoming more diverse. Now, because of the lack of state funding, citizens are being encouraged to start their own businesses, buy their own housing, and even send their children to private schools. In addition, the economic boom of eastern China has attracted people from all over the country. Wang Mei complained that the workers and getihu parents are less supportive of their children's school work. The attitudes of these people are contrasted with attitudes held by families of intellectuals and Communist Party cadres, the higher-level bureaucrats.

The Classroom

As we walked across the school yards, the children would be playing vigorously, shouting in loud voices. These tremendous bursts of energy continued to occur in the classroom, but once the teacher entered, the energy was controlled and channeled. The children sat in pairs with two moveable desks placed together in five rows. In neither school were the desks bolted to the floor. The desks are plain, made of straight boards and varnished. The tops of the desks are approximately 30 cm wide and 25 cm deep. Under the tops there was a space to keep the textbooks. All textbooks must be purchased, though the price is nominal, ranging from 1.40 to 2.45 yuan (approximately US$ .10 to .20). First graders need at least six textbooks and the total bill comes to roughly 10 yuan per semester (approximately US$ 1.10). The average urban wage in 1995 was 300 yuan per month). Under the desks, the children also store their water bottles and snacks, which they can consume between classes. It is important for children to bring their own drinking water since water is not potable. Each child comes to school with a small backpack. In it are books needed for school, as well as the snack and water bottle. The average weight of the backpack of a first grader is reported to be three kilograms (Z. Huang, 1994). There are no uniforms.

There has been some controversy in the media over excessive amounts of homework that elementary school children are expected to complete. Huang points out that the State Education Commission ruled in 1993 that first-grade children were not to be given homework. But parents in many cities demand homework and teachers comply. Teachers have also pointed out that classroom time is insufficient to cover the entire curriculum (Yu, 1992). In our observations, we never heard the explicit assignment of homework. However, we saw written work that was done at home brought to class. In other words, pupils must practice their writing skills at home to keep up.

The classrooms seem spartan as there is no great effort to provide bulletin board displays, except for a few seasonal objects that are mounted on the walls. At the front of the class over the chalkboard is a slogan of Mao Zedong, written in Chinese characters, found in almost every elementary school classroom in China:

hǎo hǎo xuéxí tiān tiān xiàng shàng
好好学习天天向上
'If you study hard and well, day by day you will excell.'

At the back of the classroom there is another large chalkboard that runs the width of the room. In both schools, thematic displays were drawn on it, making it function much like a bulletin board. Since October 1 is the National Day of China, there were beautiful chalk drawings of Tiananmen Square in Beijing enshrouded in bouquets of fireworks. The subject, *guóqīngjié* 国庆节 'National Day' was written not in Hanyu Pinyin but only in Chinese characters.

Classroom conditions are not always pleasant. At any time, a parent or another teacher can peer into the classroom through the windows. At Changjiang Road School, the classroom building was next door to a lumber yard. The whine of the chain saw interfered with teacher-student communication. At Yizhongxin School, Wang Mei's classroom was located near the lavatories. The stench would periodically waft into the room. At Changjiang Road School, where overhead projectors and tape recorders were in use, there would be frequent power failures.

At both schools, the teachers informed us that the children were rotated around the classroom about every two weeks, so that all could have the benefit of being placed near the teacher. Although we did notice some movement of students in the first six weeks, there were certain pupils who were always at the back and others who were always in the front.

The classes last for forty minutes with a five-minute break in between. At ten o'clock every morning, the whole school engages in eye exercises led by music and a prompter over the P.A. system. The children begin by massaging their nose bridge, then cheekbones, and finally forehead. The teachers walk down the aisles and help students perform the exercises correctly. These exercises were introduced by the government in the early 1950s as a way to improve children's health.

The Administration

Changjiang Road and Yizhongxin schools had a good reputation and as a result both grappled with the problem of large classes. The major differences between the schools lay in the manner of administration and methods of securing funds.

Ms. Nan Ming, vice principal of Yizhongxin School, complained about the large classes. She declared that the recommended class size for the city of Nanjing was no more than 45 students; however, most of the classes at her school had at least 55. Although this issue was presented negatively, and indeed large classes continue to be a source of administrative difficulties, high enrollment was also a source of pride. The large classes meant that the school was popular, perhaps more so than other schools. The vice principal stated that there was no shortage of schools in Nanjing. Some schools had classes with less than 20 pupils, but this was due to these schools' poor reputation. She described how families used addresses of relatives who live in reputable school neighborhoods such as the one around Yizhongxin School, thereby achieving the right to attend the school. The fact that most of the children come from families with parents who had also attended the school, suggests that in spite of the population movements due to economic changes and the competition to enter prestigious schools, this urban neighborhood in the mid-1990s was a relatively stable one. Ms. Nan Ming added that she herself had attended the school.

Class size at the key Changjiang Road School was no smaller. Each class we observed had over 55 children. This situation was also due to the competition to attend, but the competition was less among families and more among rival work units. Furthermore, pupils are tracked by ability, a practice reintroduced in the late 1970s after the Cultural Revolution (Shirk, 1979). Teachers believe it makes their work easier and cannot understand how they would deal with a mixed ability class, especially since classes are so large. We observed that the first-grade classes were made up of children with mixed ability, which indicates that tracking had not yet begun at this stage.

Every morning at 8:00, in both schools, there was a ten-minute talk by either the principal or the assistant principal. On a day with good weather, the morning ceremony was held out of doors. On other days, it was held indoors with the principal's address broadcast through the P.A. system. We noticed, in spite of the weather, that Changjiang Road School had more frequent outdoor morning ceremonies than Yizhongxin School, perhaps due to their larger playground area. These addresses usually contained moral and educational exhortations, such as to be diligent and unselfish. These addresses also included the day's announcements. One morning, the principal of Yizhongxin School, Mr. Su, spoke. The message was difficult to hear as a result of his insufficient projection and adult-oriented discourse. At the end of the address, recognizing the difficulty, Wang Mei asked the class whether they understood the message or not. One boy had done so. He stood up and paraphrased the announcement by saying that there was to be a change of schedule for second graders. He referred to the second graders in the following way:

èrniánjíde xiǎogēge hé xiǎojiějie

二年级的小哥哥和小姐姐

'the little elder brothers and little elder sisters of the second grade.'

The principal did not refer to the second graders with the same level of respect. Sometimes pupils receive opportunities to speak on the P.A. system. One day, a third grader described her trip to Hong Kong.

At Yizhongxin School, Ms. Nan Ming, the vice principal, handled the academic responsibilities, in other words, all internal administrative matters. For example, it was Ms. Nan Ming who chose the dates to hold mid-term examinations. Mr. Su, the principal, handled external affairs. His major task was raising money for the school, especially for teachers' salaries, a task principals are little accustomed to (Delany & Paine, 1991). At Changjiang Road School, however, Ms. Qian the principal, took charge of both internal and external affairs. She had no vice principal. Instead, she had consultants like Wang Lan who assisted her in administrative matters.

Since the government's "Educational Reform Decision" in 1985, educational subsidies to schools, including colleges and universities, were to be shifted largely to local governments (Delany & Paine, 1991). Even though city governments attempted to make up for the shortfall, it was insufficient to meet the demand for higher wages and improvement in facilities. To secure the needed funds, the national government allowed work units, even social service ones like schools and hospitals, to engage in profit-making businesses ("Education Essentials," 1993). In Nanjing, work units which possessed on-street property tore down walls and built two- to three-story store-front structures and then rented the spaces. In many cases the work unit itself used some of the space for their own entrepreneurial ventures, thus functioning both as landlord and vendor.

At Yizhongxin School, two shops have been constructed on either side of its gate. One shop sells sundry goods including toilet paper and ball-point pens. The other shop sells luxury snack foods including *Toblerone* chocolates and *Kraft* processed cheese. Furthermore, the first floor of the administrative building has been turned into a storeroom for the snack foods. Vans drove into the school yard, and during class time the products were loaded and unloaded. The noise of the vans did not disrupt classes.

The national government has expressed some ambivalence concerning the commercial activities of public institutions (Gong, 1993). A newspaper article ("Campaign," 1992) described regulations for commmercial activities to protect students and teachers from being exploited. In 1994, another newspaper article ("Education Reforms," 1994) called for new taxes to fund education.

In contrast, no shops have been set up on the premises of Changjiang Road School. The key school has other sources of funding. Since the school is experimental, the city provides more basic funding than to a neighborhood school. In addition, other funds come from work units who make contributions for continued access to the school.

Changjiang Road School, therefore, receives sufficient funding and support by virtue of its status as a key school. Yizhongxin School receives less than adequate funding from the same sources, that is, the city and the work units. Consequently, the school raises funds from its real estate advantages and profit-making enterprises, mainly for teachers' salaries and maintenance of the facilities.

The Teachers

Elementary school teaching is not a light job. Teachers have a five-and-a-half-day work week. Since 1994, every second Saturday has become a day off for most schools and work units. The work days, however, begin at 7:30 and continue until 4:30, with a two-and-a-half-hour break for lunch. Teachers take turns accompanying groups of children home for both the lunch period and at the end of the day. If certain children are misbehaving or having trouble, a teacher is expected to stay after school to help them. As in most parts of the world, the teacher's prestige is increased when their students do well on tests. But in addition to teaching duties, each teacher must serve as a *bānzhǔrēn* 班主任 'class teacher,' taking care of all the administrative work of the class pupils. The Chinese language teacher teaches not only language skills, but also lessons in *pǐnde* 品德 'ethics' and *láodòng* 劳动 'labor or home economics.'

While similar workloads are placed on teachers in other countries, teachers in China have had the additional load of coping with a history of official suspicion and societal scorn. The social position of teachers and other intellectuals has been precarious in twentieth century China. Reviled and therefore relegated to the "ninth stinking class" during the Cultural Revolution, intellectuals, particularly teachers, have gone through periods of persecution. Today, while overt persecution has lessened, teachers still suffer from a lack of respect. The political left suspects teachers for harboring subversive ideas; the political right ridicules people who become teachers, because in doing so they have chosen a life of poverty. In spite of the complaints by teachers about the lack of adequate compensation, this situation is not particular to the society under the Communist party. There was a pattern of teachers not being adequately paid both under the Qing dynasty and the Republican regime (Rawski, 1979).

Since 1978, the government has tried to rehabilitate the position of teachers by stressing the importance of education. It instituted a national Teachers' Day on September 15, which is given a great deal of fanfare in the media although it is not a holiday. Few concrete measures have been taken on a national scale to improve the situation of teachers. Most of the improvements, if any, have been taking place at the local level.

In the schools, the teachers themselves attempt to improve their social position by instructing pupils to respect them. At the beginning of class pupils stand and greet the teacher in unison. On Teachers' Day at Changjiang Road School, the teacher corrected the manner in which the class addressed her. Usually the pupils say:

lǎoshī nǐhǎo 老师你好 'hello teacher.'

This day, the teacher exhorted the class to say:

lǎoshī nínhǎo 老师您好 'hello honorable teacher.'

The teacher is not just another adult. She is one to whom particular respect is due.

An overt indication of the lack of social and economic improvements is the scarcity of male elementary teachers. At Changjiang Road School, there were five. At Yizhongxin School there were four. Zhu Jialong from the Jiangsu Province Education Commission, a elementary school teacher himself, was lucky to land an important administrative position. Such posts are few and the elementary teacher today is almost exclusively a women's profession (Bauer, Wang, Riley, & Zhao, 1992). This pattern is reflected in the illustrations in elementary school textbooks (Allen & Ingulsrud, 1998).

In addition to the problems of motivation and image in the teaching profession, there is also a serious lack of qualified teachers at all levels ("Train More Teachers," 1990; "Training Network," 1990). In the elementary schools, it is estimated that about 34% of elementary school teachers are unqualifed or "prequalified" (State Education Commission, 1987 in Lewin, Xu, Little, & Zheng, 1994). This situation has persisted since 1949. In the early 1950s, the lack of trained teachers was largely the result of years of war. Later, the various ideological campaigns kept qualified people away from the profession. The campaigns were utilized to ensure that all teachers, but especially elementary school ones, had the correct political background since they were responsible for developing children's minds. The Cultural Revolution focused so strongly on the ideological purity of teachers that many regretted such a choice of career (K. Cheng, 1986). Even if the teacher was politically correct, the low salaries further reduced social prestige. These patterns were already evident as early as 1951. Today, as China's economic prosperity continues to grow, teaching is still regarded as an unattractive career. Teachers colleges are failing more and more to attract capable students, as well as to attract and keep qualified faculty (Lewin, et. al., 1994; Zhang Xin, 1991).

Lack of personnel and training has continually afflicted all sectors of the educational system. As we explained in chapter one, to promote reading and writing in the elementary schools, the government in 1956 decided that Putonghua and Hanyu Pinyin were to be taught in all elementary schools. Therefore, teachers had to be trained for the task. Zhang Xiruo, then head of the Education Commission, asserted the following in his report to the Plenum of the National Writing Reform Conference in 1955 (Seybolt & Chiang, 1979):

> Aside from using correct pronunciation, it is further demanded that he (the teacher) be able to master his knowledge of pronunciation in a fairly systematic manner, understanding the correspondence between regional dialects and Peking pronunciation. . . . But teachers using the new pronunciation must grasp the correspondences between the dialect of their own region and Peking pronunciation, since only in this way will it be easy for the teachers to guide the people of that region to a mastery of Peking pronunciation. (p. 71)

Acquiring this kind of linguistic skill was not an easy task for many teachers (Yin & Baldauf, 1990). Large numbers of teachers needed special training, including consciousness-raising as to the importance of learning Putonghua and Hanyu Pinyin. The government actively identified model teachers who could help train others and established special schools to experiment with teaching methods and materials. In addition, a special propaganda unit to spread Putonghua was also created in order to counter the hostility towards the language reforms. Zhu Jialong's office in the Jiangsu Province Education Commission continues the work of Putonghua promotion.

Today, these issues persist with many teachers still lacking insufficient training. As a result, opportunities for teachers to continue their education have been provided in many localities. They can attend evening classes or short courses during their vacation periods. They are also urged to watch model teachers in their schools or go to demonstration classes given by model teachers at other schools. Throughout our observations, we regularly saw teachers visiting Changjiang Road School for demonstration classes, as well as individual teachers sitting in on Hanyu Pinyin lessons in both schools. The training received by a majority of teachers at both schools is from normal middle schools, meaning teacher-training high schools. Some teachers come from normal colleges, generally ones with two-year programs. But in spite of the variety of academic backgrounds, all must take continuing education courses. Some of the courses are required for all teachers, and others are optional for teachers working toward higher levels of certification. Teachers can study by correspondence programs offered by Nanjing Normal University or the Television University (电视大学).

Because of the leveling off of public funds for education, many schools like Yizhongxin School are forced to raise money on their own. In some areas of China, even the small government subsidies for teachers' salaries were redirected to other projects (Gong, 1993). Stopping short of charging tuition, many schools have begun charging a variety of fees. These fees have been declared illegal, but as the government is not in a position to provide additional funding, there is little that the authorities can do to control this trend ("State Bans," 1993). Since most pupils in urban schools come from one-child families, the fees are collected with little difficulty. Moreover, in a large class of more than 50 pupils, each of whom is an only child, parents offer gifts to the teacher so that their child is given attention. Stiff competition in the schools begins as early as first grade, so parents make sure that the teacher is well satisfied.

The power of the teacher over the life of the pupil is further enhanced by the policy of having a teacher stay with the same class for all six years of primary school, a general policy in the neighborhood school, but not enforced in a rigid way. In the key school, the opposite policy was taken. Teachers changed frequently from day to day. In the first-grade Yuwen classes, for example, a different teacher could appear for each day of the week.

In spite of the economic and status problems that teachers face—problems that are covered frequently in the media and come up often in conversations with teachers—our observations have led us to believe that the social position of urban elementary school teachers is not as low as it may seem. The fact is, teachers are not powerless. They do have influence over the kind and amount of attention that they will provide their pupils. Concerned parents, therefore, realize the importance of giving attention to their child's teacher as well.

The elementary school teachers at both schools, for example, are well-dressed. The teachers at Changjiang Road School were well-dressed in 1990 and the teachers at Yizhongxin School were even more so in 1993. Our observations in both schools took place in the warm months of September and October. During that time, we noticed that ten days can go by without a repeat in outfit. In contrast, middle school teachers and our colleagues at the university were far less concerned about their attire. We have not found any simple explanations of this phenomenon, but perhaps the access that elementary school teachers have to the most socially mobile of groups today, that is young families, has contributed to changing values.

The Parents

In this study we have focused on the classroom; consequently, we did not interview parents. This choice, however, does not diminish the importance of the parents' role in the literacy acquisition process both in emergent literacy and after the child enters school. Parents are usually the child's first teacher. For example, Wang Mei mentioned that most parents teach their children to write their names in Chinese characters. This teaching role is further emphasized by the attitude teachers take toward individual pupils. Pupils who received help at home were held in higher regard by the teacher.

Every morning the younger children arrive at school accompanied by their parents. At Changjiang Road School most children arrive by bicycle as their families generally do not live in the neighborhood. Recently, at both schools, more and more children are being driven to school in automobiles. In Changchun, northeast China, for instance, car transport to school has caused such traffic snarls, newspapers report schools forbidding parents to drive their children to school ("Kids Scold," 1993).

Wang Mei consistently emphasized the role of parents rather than the role of individual ability as an indicator for academic achievement. In our conversations with her concerning the pupils, the focus tends to be, as it is among teachers around the world, not on the average student, but on the extremes—the achievers and the under-achievers. For the achievers, there were comments about social class or privilege. The father is an official. The mother is preparing to travel overseas. For the non-achievers, the reasons were also about class and privilege: the parents are running a private business. The girl lives with her father. The parents are always fighting. The parents are divorced, so the boy lives with his grandparents. For a child to cope in a class of over 50 other children, support from home, both psychologically and academically, is essential.

Occasionally, Wang Mei shared with us the written work that the pupils had completed in class. At this early stage, the writing consisted of practice in copying models of alphabet shapes as well as dictation quizzes. After correcting the dictations, she would frequently have pupils take their papers home. There they would show them to their parents and then have the papers signed by them. This is done to hold parents responsible for their child's performance (Yu, 1992). When asked if the pupils actually bring them back to class, Wang Mei replied that about 8 out of 55 forget to bring them back. She said one father was so angry, he ripped the paper and did not even bother to tape it up, so the child returned the scraps. Parental expectations can be high. One survey showed that 60% of parents questioned had beaten their child over what they regarded as poor academic performance ("60% Beaten," 1992). In contrast, one mother wrote a long note on the back of her child's quiz thanking and extolling the work of the teacher. Judging from the glee with which the teacher recounted to us this detail, we were given the impression that it is a clever parent who keeps the teacher happy.

Even though parents are seen as children's first reading teachers, in urban China, kindergarten teachers precede elementary school teachers. It was only after our initial observations at Changjiang Road School that we discovered that children came to school prepared. We discussed this phenomenon with our contacts in the Jiangsu Province Education Commission. They insisted that there was no formal preschool training in the reading and writing of Hanyu Pinyin. However, we later discovered that children came to school with knowledge of the alphabet, some Chinese characters, as well as some English. However, the most important clue for their having been trained lay in the old-fashioned pronunciation of individual Hanyu Pinyin letters. As will be described in detail in chapter four, the method used today to link sound and symbol is one based on phonics, that is, individual sounds. The older method is based on syllables.

At Changjiang Road School, the explanation for the children's readiness was the parents' coaching at home. Since couples are limited to one child, their child's academic achievement tends to be a matter of great concern. We assumed many parents taught the children Hanyu Pinyin in the same way that they had learned it, which is through syllables. The fast pace of the class, especially at

Changjiang Road School, also led us to believe that teachers depended on parental coaching. Material not introduced by the teacher, for example, was elicited from the class, giving the impression that the good student is one who already knows textbook material that the class has yet to cover. Coaching children can be demanding for parents. They are reported to take sick leave to help their children prepare for examinations. Many parents hire college students to tutor even preschool children (Bo, 1991; Yu, 1992).

After our observations at Changjiang Road School in 1990, we casually inquired about how preschool children are prepared for school. A colleague at Nanjing University who had a kindergarten-aged son mentioned that at the university kindergarten, Hanyu Pinyin classes were indeed being conducted. Through her we gained entry to the kindergarten to observe Hanyu Pinyin classes. The class was held for one hour, once a week on Fridays for twelve weeks, from the beginning of April until the beginning of July. These were the final weeks of preschool for the children. We were able to observe this once-a-week lesson in 1991 and in 1992.

These reading classes were not unique to this particular kindergarten that was attached to a major university. Evidence of the widespread existence of these lessons in the Nanjing area lay in the published Hanyu Pinyin workbooks specifically designed for kindergartens. These workbooks were published under the auspices of the Jiangsu Province Education Commission. Why the officials denied the existence of such lessons remains for us a mystery.

The Kindergarten

Nanjing University Kindergarten (南京大学幼儿园) was well equipped with a two-story concrete classroom building, and large playground with a variety of playground equipment. Although the kindergarten ran a three-year program (the daycare center for infants was located elsewhere), the kindergarten provided a bed for each child. Also, unlike the school where the children went home for lunch, the kindergarten children had lunch at school. Parents bring their children by bicycle in the morning before work (between 7:30 and 8:00 a.m.) and stop by after work to pick them up.

The children were divided into classes of 25 to 30 pupils each. The teachers had responsibilities for individual classes, but they also shared teaching responsibilities across classes. Tobin, Wu, and Davidson (1989) who studied Chinese kindergartens, found that there was a range of educational attainment among the teachers. In their study, they mentioned that in a university-attached kindergarten in Beijing, all the teachers had two years of tertiary education. They mentioned that elsewhere in China, most teachers were graduates of normal high schools or were untrained adults. Although we were unable to obtain precise information concerning the teachers' training, we found that even at the university-attached kindergarten, the academic backgrounds of the teachers were mixed. The kindergarten teachers, particularly in the Hanyu Pinyin lessons, were far less self-confident than the elementary school teachers, and their teaching methodology did not reflect current trends.

The once-a-week Hanyu Pinyin lesson lasted 40 minutes. The teacher began by writing three or four letters on the chalkboard. After that she modeled the sounds. In her modeling, she employed the older, syllabic method of modeling sounds, for example, [buo] instead of [bə], which provided the clue as to why children in first grade were pronouncing sounds in this manner. Then the teacher presented vocabulary that used the sounds. Vocabulary was not elicited; instead the children repeated the teacher-initiated vocabulary. This oral practice, however, was very short, lasting only about ten minutes. The rest of the time was spent on writing.

At the beginning of the writing session, the teacher handed the stack of workbooks, issued by the Jiangsu Province Education Commission, to one boy. On the back of each workbook was the name of the child written in Chinese characters. This five-year-old was able to pass out correctly the workbooks to each of his 25 classmates. The teacher mentioned that his parents had taught him to read. In the workbook, there were rows of small boxes. At the top of each page were three alphabetical letters. Below each letter, there was a dotted-line outline of the letters provided so that the children could trace the proper shapes. Below the dotted outlines were empty boxes for the children to practice writing by filling them in. The teacher went around urging the children to concentrate and follow the outlines as closely as possible. The task for a single session involved filling in one page, thus practicing three letters. Some children finished early while others did not finish in the allotted 25 minutes.

Based on coaching at home and lessons at kindergarten, the urban child in China enters grade one with a knowledge of the Roman letters and the sounds associated with them. While the elementary school teachers assume this knowledge in terms of curriculum pacing, they start at the very beginning as if the children do not possess any knowledge of Hanyu Pinyin.

Summary

The two schools that we studied in Nanjing were considered good schools. In spite of their exceptional reputation, these schools had large classes. The key school even had classes of 55 children or over. In spite of the often exemplary teaching performance on the part of the teachers, attention to the many individual needs could not be carried out in such large-class situations. We observed children who, with more individual assistance, could have perhaps overcome some of the reading and writing difficulties they were encountering. Teachers cannot provide the necessary attention to such large numbers and widely diverse groups of children. The problem of large classes, however, is not unique to urban China but exists in Japan as well as the United States. The assumption remains that by improving the student-teacher ratio, the efforts of schools will meet with increased success.

The question remains as to why parents flocked to these schools despite the large classes. For the key school, its popularity is understandable due to its academic status. For the neighborhood school, there were no particular external attributes that would necessarily attract parents. We were informed that there was no shortage of schools in Nanjing. Still, the ones with more prestige attracted more than their quota. The basis for the school's prestige, from our observations, lay in the teachers themselves. They were seen to do a good job. Moreover, the attitudes that the teachers maintained, in both schools, toward their profession were positive. We have described how the teaching profession since the late 1950s has suffered for ideological reasons. Today, there is less suspicion of teachers but they tend to be underpaid, thus interpreting the manner in which they are compensated as being less valued in society. Indeed, among our students at the undergraduate and graduate levels who were preparing to become English teachers, morale was low, in spite of English education being a high growth discipline. In contrast, the elementary school teachers we observed seemed to be paid adequately. Their confident attitude was reflected in their attire and the way they presented themselves.

A positive school environment was possible, in the mid-1990s, because of the efforts of the administration at both schools. The principals were able to procure more funds than the alloted subsidy from the city. At Changjiang Road School, patronage was encouraged from the work units that were interested in maintaining a connection with the school. At Yizhongxin School, the principal worked full-time in promoting money-making schemes so that the school could have adequate funds. Their success in these ventures resulted in keeping good teachers, maintaining the facilities, and thus building their reputation among parents.

The school's reputation, therefore, was viewed by parents as more important than the large class sizes. The teachers we interviewed in Nanjing were forthright in pointing out that children cannot achieve the goals of literacy acquisition simply by relying on classroom instruction. Children, if they are to be successful in terms of the curriculum and among their peers, need help from home. Our observations in the neighborhood school, even with the demographic advantages, lead us to conclude that assistance from home is very much a case-by-case situation. Some children are neglected while others are pampered with attention. Despite the variety of family environments even for the single children, the teachers report that the majority are receiving some kind of help.

Changjiang Road School

Yizhongxing School

A first grade classroom

A display for National Day on the chalkboard at the back of the classroom

School businesses

Going to school

Slogans to promote the use of Putonghua

Chinese script word boundaries applied to English

Chapter Three
Learning to Speak Putonghua

The initial classroom task of the Chinese first grader is learning to speak. Obviously, each child does come to school already speaking Chinese. But as we described in chapter one, the language the child learns at home is often not the same as the language taught at school. Indeed, the duration of the lessons introducing Putonghua through the Hanyu Pinyin alphabet varies with the extent of the difference between the local variety and Putonghua. The lessons can last as long as 12 weeks in certain dialect group areas such as in Cantonese-speaking Guangdong Province.

In Nanjing the lessons do not last this long. At the key school, five weeks were allocated, and at the neighborhood school, six and a half weeks. The shorter time in Nanjing is due to the nature of the local dialect, a variety of Southern Mandarin which is part of the Northern Chinese dialect group. Seen in the light of China's vast linguistic variation, Nanjinghua is a dialect that does not deviate greatly from Putonghua. The relationship might be compared to the difference between the English spoken in corporate Chicago along Michigan Avenue and the English spoken in rural Queensland, west of Cairns.

Wang Lan, consultant at Changjiang Road School (the key school), reported how difficult it was for one of her former teacher trainees to teach Putonghua in Shenzhen, a sprawling special economic zone bordering Hong Kong.

The first grade class in this city represents not only the local variety of Cantonese, but varieties from dialect groups all over China. The Nanjing school teacher can, at least, expect a high degree of linguistic homogeneity in her classroom.

At both Changjiang Road and Yizhongxin Schools, before they begin school, between August 16 and 22, there is a week of orientation for first graders. During this time they are taught to sit still, sit up straight with arms folded over on the desk, raise their hands from the elbow up when they want to speak, and arrange their things properly on their desks. Books are neatly stacked together and placed at the top right-hand corner of the desk. Although first grade requires adjustments to school life, regimentation of this kind is not new. As has been described in chapter two, most urban children experience similar regimentation for three years in kindergarten. The major difference from the kindergarten setting, according to our observations, is the larger classes, and the resulting reduction of personal attention and the demand for more sharing. Most urban children are already accustomed to Putonghua as the medium of instruction as it is also spoken in the kindergartens.

Teachers at both schools begin the academic curriculum with lessons in Putonghua. They do so by exhorting the importance of the common language for China: Putonghua provides the means by which everyone in the nation communicates. The teachers further point out that learning Hanyu Pinyin will allow children to recognize print and help them learn Chinese characters. In addition to these practical benefits of learning Putonghua and Hanyu Pinyin, there is an aesthetic value attached to the common language. Putonghua is *piǎoliang* 漂亮 'beautiful' and it is *hǎotīng* 好听 'sounds nice.' Nanjinghua, on the other hand, is *bùhǎotīng* 不好听 'doesn't sound nice.'

The Representation of Putonghua

The Hanyu Pinyin alphabet represents Putonghua phonemically. It is unlike the popular Hepburn romanization for Japanese that is based on the English phonemic system. In Tables A1 and A2 in the Appendix, we compare the Hanyu Pinyin alphabetic system with the International Phonetic Alphabet and the still-popular Wade-Giles system for Chinese romanization. We do so by offering a list of initial and final components for Putonghua syllables. This is a traditional way of organizing Chinese sounds, beginning with the initial components of syllables (most often consonants) and final components of syllables (most often vowels). We also include examples of how these components might be pronounced in English. We caution that many of the examples are only approximations. Information for the lists was drawn primarily from *Mathews' Chinese-English dictionary* (1943) and *A concise Chinese-English dictionary* (1991).

One of the more confusing aspects of the Hanyu Pinyin system is the rules governing the distinction between the letters q and ch, x and sh, and j and zh. The q sound is pronounced with the middle of the tongue (velar affricate), and the ch sound is pronounced with the tip of the tongue (post-alveolar affricate). The distinction between x (velar fricative) and sh (post-alveolar fricative) is also the same. Both the j and the zh sounds are pronounced with the tip of the tongue (voiced alveolar affricate). The letters q, j, and x occur only with high tense vowels and umlauts. They are in complementary distribution with ch and sh which occur with high lax vowels and the middle and lower vowels. The problem is that orthographically they all appear in combination with both i and u. The reader must remember that for q, j, and x, i is tense as in "he" while i is lax for ch, sh, and zh as in "it." The u sound is umlauted for q and x, while it is simply rounded for ch, sh, and zh as in "suit."

In the tables we have not indicated tones. In Chinese, tones are phonemic and in Putonghua there are four tones plus syllables that have no tones. The first tone is level " ¯." The second is rising " ´." The third tone is falling and rising " ˇ." Finally the fourth tone is falling sharply " ˋ." In Hanyu Pinyin, tone is indicated in each syllable with the diacritic over a vowel. Regarding the selection of which vowel, some rules (Peng, 1984) are provided in Table 7. The rules are ordered hierarchically:

Table 7

Rules for Placing Tone Diacritics in Hanyu Pinyin

1.	The tone diacritic is always placed over a vowel.	
2.	The tone diacritic is always placed over the vowel "a."	
3.	The tone diacritic is placed over the vowel "o" or "e" if "a" does not appear.	
4.	The tone diacritic is placed over the second vowel when the vowels "i" and "u" appear together.	

The Putonghua Lesson

At the beginning of class, the chalkboard has been prepared beforehand with the material that is to be covered. The teacher also has prepared various sizes of slates on which vocabulary items and individual letters, as well as groups of letters, are written. Both sides of the slates can be used. The top of the slate hooks backwards and the bottom of the slate hooks forward, thus allowing the slates to be hung down in a chain from the top of the chalkboard.

When the bell rings, the children rush in and take their places at their desks. There are two pupils at each desk. When the classmates have found their places, the class monitor, a designated pupil to serve as a leader, stands up and shouts:

qǐlì 起立 'stand up.'

The whole class stands, and then, together with the monitor, bows toward the teacher saying,

lǎoshī nǐhǎo 老师你好 'hello teacher.'

The teacher responds,

xuésheng nǐhǎo 学生你好 'hello students.'

This is a formal moment in the lesson, for the teacher rarely addresses the pupils as *xuésheng* 学生 'students.' Instead, she usually calls them *xiǎopéngyou* 小朋友 'little friends.'

The teacher introduces the lesson by telling the pupils what they are to study. For example, in the first lesson, the vowels a, i, u, o are introduced. The illustration from the textbook depicts a physician with a tongue depressor asking a child to say [a---h]. The teacher points to the letter on the board and then vocally models the sound. Then the class repeats chorally. After that, individual pupils are called on to say the sound. When they are called upon, each stands up and then produces the sound.

It is up to this point that both schools follow the same procedure. From then on there is a temporary divergence. At Changjiang Road School, teachers use an overhead projector. After initial repetition of the sound, the teacher shows a transparency depicting a cross section of the mouth indicating the position of the tongue, so that graphically the pupils can observe the point of articulation—much in the same way that pronunciation lessons are conducted in foreign language classes.

On the other hand at Yizhongxin school, Wang Mei quickly explains the place and manner of articulation without visual aids, but then follows the explanation with a rhyme for each sound. The example rhyme below explains the manner of vowel production:

zuǐba yuán yuán o-o-o
嘴巴圆圆 喔 - 喔 - 喔
'both lips round round o-o-o'

yáchǐ duìzhì i-i-i
牙齿对峙 咿 - 咿 - 咿
'up by the teeth i-i-i'

zuǐba zhāngdà a-a-a
嘴巴张大 啊 - 啊 - 啊
'lips open wide a-a-a'

zuĭba biănbiăn e-e-e

嘴巴扁扁 哦－哦－哦

'lips open slightly e-e-e'

Although these rhymes are usually repeated chorally, Wang Mei often selects two pupils and asks them to come forward. Once in front of the class, she asks them to face each other and repeat the rhymes while each watches the other's lips. Then she asks the whole class to stand and face their partners. The teacher had to go through the class to make sure the pupils were physically facing each other. We did not observe any pupil correcting another pupil, but this peer monitoring involves participation of all pupils at the same time, hopefully encouraging the pupils to pronounce sounds correctly.

Phonemic tone in Hanyu Pinyin is indicated by one of four diacritic symbols (‾ ‵ ‶ ‵) placed over a vowel in each syllable. When the syllables are taught, the teacher writes the syllable on the board and then elicits vocabulary. It is at this point that the proper listening and proper pronunciation are reinforced. For instance, if the teacher has presented the syllable *bà*, then individual pupils can offer sample vocabulary by saying:

bàba de bà 爸爸的 bà 'bà for bàba 'father''

Pupils guess the vocabulary and the teacher judges whether their guesses are correct or incorrect depending on articulation and tone.

Wang Mei at Yizhongxin School encourages her pupils to tell stories both when she introduces new sounds and then later when eliciting vocabulary. There was one particular girl who was frequently ready to tell a story and so the teacher regularly called on her. Most of the time her stories were long, often lasting for several minutes. She was once reprimanded for rambling and was instructed to tell shorter stories, but she continued to tell long ones. Whenever she told a story, other pupils tended to lose interest and some began to play around. The pupils were inclined to listen only to the teacher and not to each other, a behavior that exists among university students as well. In Table 8, the basic Putonghua lesson is summarized.

Table 8

Summary of a Putonghua Lesson

1.	Sounds are introduced together with individual letters. Chalkboards, slates, and overhead transparencies are used. a. Pupils see the shapes of letters with mnemonic devices. b. Pupils hear the sounds and repeat after teacher. c. Teacher presents the place and manner of articulation by means of a transparency or uses a rhyme to help young children remember.
2.	Consonants and vowels are linked to make syllables.
3.	Tone diacritics are added to the syllables.
4.	Together with tone and syllable, examples for vocabulary are elicited.
5.	Incorrect vocabulary examples are repaired and accurate examples are praised.

Speaking Practice

Implicit in the content of the lesson above, is the use of phonics to link sound and symbol. The use of phonics is described in chapter four in relation to learning the alphabet. The teaching of phonics also involves speaking practice, but we observed that the most common method, choral repetition, created problems that phonics learning should have solved. For a class of over 50 children who need to be occupied if their attention is to be focused, choral repetition is a frequently used teaching technique. When the whole class repeats, the pace slows down and drags. The dragging pace phenomenon existed in both schools, as it does in foreign language classes around the world when choral repetition is used. At Changjiang Road School, for instance, instead of a short [bə] pupils would often say [buoa-].

When this happened at Changjiang Road School, the consultant, Wang Lan who would also be observing, interrupted the class by speaking up from the back of the classroom. She encouraged the teacher to keep up the pace. Other teachers interspersed the choral repetition with individual repetition and repetition by rows. Wang Mei, while frequently scolding the class for dragging the pace, also conducted a special kind of exercise to deal with group pace. This was called the

72

train drill. She challenged the class:

shî shúide huǒchē kāide kuài?
是谁的火车开的快？
'Whose train can go the fastest?'

The class responded:

wǒmende huǒchē kāide kuài!
我们的火车开的快！
'Our train goes the fastest!'

    Each train consists of a row of desks stretching from the teacher to the back of the classroom. Two desks are placed together, thus forming four rows in the classroom. But for the train drill, the eight rows compete against each other for even pace and accurate pronunciation. The teacher says the word to the first pupil and then the second one repeats it right after the first one and so on. Those that break the chain are singled out and asked to repeat again. As this drill goes on, the focus of the teacher shifts more to the rhythm of the group and less to the pronunciation of the syllable.

    Forms of modeling include the use of a piece of paper to illustrate aspiration. For instance, to distinguish between p and b, the teacher held a piece of paper in front of her mouth. It moved when she said p and did not when she said b. The children imitated her, by holding their hands in front of their mouths. At Changjiang Road School as mentioned earlier, overhead transparencies were used illustrating the points of articulation. When the sounds n and l were introduced, the teacher explained that the place of articulation was the same, but the manner of articulation was different. For n the air goes through the nose while for l the air goes through two sides of the tongue. Then she asked the class to hold their nose and say [lə, lə, lə]. Wang Mei at Yizhongxin School depended a great deal on her explanations, but by doing so she developed some creative techniques. She also asked the class hold their noses to practice l, but in fact when the class practiced n many pupils were saying [l]. When she introduced the umlaut **ü**, she asked the class:

zuǐba zěnmezhāng? 嘴巴怎么张？'How do you shape the lips?'

She answered her own question:

zuǐba tūchūlai. 嘴巴突出来。'By sticking them out.'

Then she picked up the pointer and pretended to play the flute.

At other times, Wang Mei would ask a pupil to come to the front and act as teacher. The pupil, with pointer in hand, lead the class in choral repetition. The children literally jumped up and down with excitement for a chance to be teacher. She often used pupils as models, more frequently than teachers at Changjiang Road School and asked certain ones quite regularly. When a pupil modeled correctly she responded,

hěnhǎo 很好 'very good.'

Sometimes, before she made a comment, she would ask the class how the pupil modeled the sound,

hǎo bù hǎo? 好不好？'Is it good or bad?'

Most often the response was *hǎo* 好 'good' or *hǎode* 好的 'good one.' Other positive teacher responses included:

duì 对 'correct'
bùcuò 不错 'not bad'
cōngming 聪明 'brilliant'
zhēngè 真个 'accurate'
zhēnhǎo 真好 'really good'

fēichánghǎo 非常好 'extremely good'

hěnnénggàn 很能干 'very capable'

hěnyǒnggǎn 很勇敢 'very courageous'

Some negative reactions by the teacher included:

nǐ bùtīng 你不听 'you're not listening'

nǐ bùyào nòng 你不要弄 'don't fool around'

nǐ shì huàidàn 你是坏蛋 'you're a bad egg'

To get the attention of the class, teachers would frequently bang the pointer on the desk. To get the attention of individuals, teachers often confiscate pencil cases and books. That meant the scolding came later, after class, when the pupil went up to redeem the articles. Some of the phrases used to draw the attention of the class to the teacher included:

yī èr 一二 'one two'

yǎnjing kàn lǎoshī 眼睛看老师 'look at the teacher'

The Interference of Dialect

In both schools, the teachers readily acknowledged that there were certain sounds particularly difficult for the children because of the influence of the local Nanjing dialect. The most obvious difficulty is the Putonghua phonemic distinction between [n] and [l], two sounds that locally occur in free variation. The interchangeability of [n] and [l] exists widely in South China, as described in chapter one, and is not a unique feature of Nanjing speech. Some examples of this free variation that we documented from the children's speech include the pronunciation of the following examples:

nǎinai 奶奶 'grandmother' as [lailai]

nǎli 哪里 'where' as [lali].

nuǒmǐ 糯米 'glutinous rice' as [luomi].

lúnchuán 轮船 'steamship' as [nuntṣuan].

As one can see, there are more examples of [n] —> [l] than of [l] —> [n], although both patterns exist. The teachers spend extra time on these sounds. After much practice with minimal pair drills and repetition of sounds, the children can distinguish in the exercises between [n] and [l], but as soon as they spoke freely in more communicative activities such as in vocabulary elicitation, the distinctions ceased to exist.

There are other well-known difficulties. In both schools, the children had difficulty in distinguishing the following pairs: z-zh, c-ch, and s-sh. In Nanjing and in the Wu dialect group areas, there are usually no retroflex sounds. The post-alveolar fricative sh is pronounced as [s] and and the two post-alveolar affricates, ch and zh, are pronounced [ts'] and [ts] respectively. Consequently, adults, as well as the children in the classroom, will say [huots'itsan] instead of huǒchēzhàn 火车站 'train station,' or [saŋhai] for Shanghai. The children are not unaware of these distinctions. There are examples of hypercorrection where pupils overgeneralize on the retroflex sounds where it is unnecessary. For example, some pupils pronounced sìrén 四人 'four people' as [ṣirɛn].

There are less-known dialect interference difficulties that appeared in the classroom. The alveolar affricate c seemed especially difficult for the children to pronounce. When introduced in lesson 7 of the textbook as part of a contrasting set z-c-s, some pupils did not make any distinction between these sounds, so that all three sounded the same. Later on in lesson 11, the alveolar stop t is contrasted with the alveolar affricate c in a minimal pair:

chītáo 吃桃 'eat peach'
chīcǎo 吃草 'eat grass.'

Many children pronounced both táo and cǎo beginning with c. Through the din of choral repetition, perhaps the affricate, not the stop, was the sound that was heard best. Then again, *cǎihóng* 彩虹 'rainbow' was pronunced as [taihoŋ]. When we inquired about this difficulty, a teacher at Changjiang Road School mentioned that the children's inablity to make a distinction between t and c is a result also of interference from the Nanjing dialect but we have no independent verification that this might be the case.

When the sounds in and ing are introduced, these nasal sounds are distinguished by place of articulation: the dental and velar. Many pupils in both schools had difficulty hearing this difference and thus could not produce the distinction. At Changjiang Road School, overhead transparencies demonstrated where the tongue touches the oral cavity in the velar and dental positions. To emphasize the difference between these two sounds, the teachers highly exaggerated both sounds so that a syllable like *ying* sounded like [jijuŋ] or [jijoŋ] that included an extra palatal glide. The pupils were expected to repeat this exaggerated pronunciation whether in isolation or in a word. If they did not do so, they were reprimanded. Many pupils were confused and unable to produce the exaggerated sounds. For instance, when one boy was asked to pronounce the syllable *ying,* he kept on saying *ying* correctly even though the teacher stood beside him and asked him to say [jijoŋ]. Finally she gave up and he sat down, looking very puzzled. Later, when the class was asked to repeat the word *qīngtíng* 蜻蜓 'dragonfly,' the responses varied and included no nasalization as in [tɕintijou], slight nasalization as in [tɕingtiŋ], and exaggerated nasalization as in [tɕintijoŋ]. When she heard [tɕintijou] the teacher scolded the pupils, saying this was the Nanjing dialect and thus was not acceptable. Again we could not find any verification for this being the case. Consequently we began to sense that "Nanjinghua" was used as a convenient dustbin for all non-standard sounds whether they were dialect-based or produced by developmental trial and error.

Other nasal contrasts such as an-ang and en-eng-ong were highly exaggerated by the teachers we observed at Changjiang Road School. One explanation for this exaggeration might lie in the fact that the school was a model school and the teachers were constantly supervised and openly criticized in the classroom. As a result, they were under a great deal more pressure than teachers in other schools to perform in specified ways. Although this emphasis on the nasals appeared to be extreme and the children seemed confused by it, the teachers were required to follow the directives of consultants like Wang Lan. At the neighborhood school, Wang Mei was freer to trust her own judgement.

Some of the difficulties appear to come from the textbook itself. The two sets of sounds are presented one after the other, in lessons 7 and 8: Lesson 7 introduces z-c-s while lesson 8 presents zh-ch-sh. At Yizhongxin School we were able regularly to see the dictation papers. The weaker pupils wrote z-c-s for zh-ch-sh or visa versa, indicating that they were unable to distinguish between the sounds.

The most difficult lesson we observed at Yizhongxin School was lesson 5, the introduction of the velars g-k-h. Wang Mei began the lesson in her usual way by reviewing the previous lesson's sounds and then introduced the new set by pointing out the similarity between the illustration in the textbook and the shape of the letter. Next she modeled the sounds, with the pupils imitating her. In spite of this technique, some pupils found it very difficult to distinguish between the three sounds. When pronounced in isolation, the children were able to pronounce each of the three velar sounds. But as soon as they had to practice all three and try to distinguish between them, they were unable to do so. For instance, when asked to read a syllable on a slate, one pupil's response was [ge] instead of *he* or [bu] instead of *hu*. Perhaps with the latter, the pupils might have visually confused the letters h and b and so said [bu] instead of *hu* During the lesson, Wang Mei asked individual pupils to pronounce *ku* which was written on a slate, but after six children had failed to do so, she gave up and went back to modeling the sounds and having the whole class repeat after her. Later, when she showed *gu* on a slate and asked the pupils as a class to pronounce it, many said [bu].

This mistake resulted in sharp scolding. Clearly, the teacher and the pupils were frustrated by this set of sounds. Even though the teacher went down the rows and asked every child to pronounce *gu* there were many who still persisted in saying [bu]. Perhaps it is at this point where visual aids might have helped. Since the velar sounds are produced by the back of the tongue, children cannot see how the teacher is forming them. Such kinds of difficulties with velar sounds were not observed at Changjiang Road School where overhead transparencies were used in illustrating the points of articulation.

Tones and Standard Vocabulary

Tone in Chinese is phonemic. That means two words with the same pronunciation can have different meanings depending on the tone. The classic example is the one syllable word *ma*: *mā* 马 'horse,' *má* 妈 'mother,' *mǎ* 麻 'hemp,' *mà* 骂 'curse,' exemplifying the four tones of Putonghua. There are some syllables that receive no tones especially in the position of second or third syllables in a compound. One example that fits with the series above is the question morpheme, *ma* 吗 as in *hěn guìma?* 很贵吗? 'is it very expensive?'

Typically, foreign language learners of Chinese complain that the second tone, the rising one, is most difficult to hear and produce. From our observations of first grade pupils, the second tone also seems to be most difficult. The concept of tones is introduced immediately after the first five vowels have been taught. Each vowel sound is then practiced with a tone. Although the class could repeat most of the vowel sounds in the four tones accurately, the second and third tone for the letter o seemed the most problematic.

Wang Mei, however, claims that it is the third tone (the falling and rising) that is most difficult for the children. Anticipating this difficulty, Ms. Wang dealt with the third tone in a positive manner by announcing to the class:

dìsānshēng shì zuì piàoliangde

第三声是最漂亮的

'The third tone sounds the prettiest.'

When the children had to pronounce letters or syllables with different tone marks, they often could not make a distinction between the second and third tones. The second tone tended to sound the same as the third tone and so there would be no difference, for example, between *bú* and *bǔ*, *pá* and *pǎ*, and *hé* and *hě* The pupils' difficulty in identifying these tones became particularly apparent when the teachers elicited vocabulary to illustrate tones, especially the second tone. The teacher held a slate with a syllable such as *yí* and pupils gave examples of words containing the syllable with the proper tone as in *mǎyǐ* 蚂蚁 'ant.' Often words were offered that had the wrong tone. For instance, one child responded,

yīfu de yi 衣服的*yi* 'the *yi* for "clothes".'

This answer was incorrect as *yi* in this lexical item is pronounced with the first tone not the third tone which happened to be the topic of the moment. Moreover, in the Hanyu Pinyin class, when no tone is indicated, it is assumed to be the first tone, even though there are syllables with no tone. The fourth tone also caused some difficulties because it is pronounced more loudly than the other tones.

One possible explanation for the difficulties is the outcome of certain tone combinations. There is the phenomenon called tone sandhi. In Putonghua, when two syllables with the third tone occur consecutively, the first syllable of the compound takes on the second tone. For example, the word *hénhǎo* 很好 'very good' has two consecutive syllables with the third tone. However, the word is actually pronounced as *hénhǎa* We are not sure that tone sandhi was a factor in the children's difficulties at this stage. Most of the pronunciation practice was done with only one and two syllable words. As a result, there were few occasions where tone sandhi occurred.

To reinforce the pronunciation, Wang Mei used the *bǐbǐkàn* 比比看 'look and compare' game. Two pupils would be chosen, each in different rows. After they stood up she would show a flashcard of a syllable or word and ask each to pronounce it. The one who could pronounce it quicker and more accurately was the winner. Then the winner would nominate the next person to compete with. Whenever the teacher announced *bǐbǐkàn* the pupils would buzz with excitement.

Although the training in tones is the last phonemic element to be added to the spoken language, the semantic and stylistic fine-tuning is no easy task. Sociolinguistic studies have suggested most people will fine-tune their speech, whether it is toward a standard variety or toward a non-standard vernacular throughout their lives. In the case of Putonghua training in the schools, the stylistic fine-tuning is primarily helping the children develop a sense of what kind of speech is appropriate in school.

In lesson 6 of the textbook, the voiceless velar fricative x is introduced. In the vocabulary section of the lesson a teacher at Changjiang Road School used one of us as classroom realia. She pointed to John's beard and asked the class what it was. They all responded:

hǘzi 胡子.

However, the teacher said that word was too informal. Instead, beards should be called:

hǘxū 胡须.

Upon consultation with other Chinese informants, there was disagreement with the teacher's sense of register. According to them, *hǘzi* is acceptable even in formal speech. But then again, the lesson was on the letter x. The teacher, like many of the rest of us who are language teachers, tended to prioritize structure as it appears in the curriculum over the real-life use of the language.

Kinship terms were corrected to standard and adult forms. For instance, *xiǎomōba* 'little brother' was corrected to *xiǎodīdi* 小弟弟. *nǎinai* 奶奶 'grandmother' and *pópo* 婆婆 'paternal grandmother' were corrected in favor of *zūmu* 祖母. For the sound yǔ there was *yǔtou* 芋头 'sweet potato,' but the pupils were told this was *nánfānghuà* 南方话 'southern speech' and that sweet potatoes are called *dìgua* 地瓜.

The children we observed were made aware that Nanjing dialect was non-standard and unacceptable in the classroom and that they were required to learn a more formal code. Yet the use of standard and non-standard language was not so clear-cut. This is because all the teachers we observed continually slipped into the Nanjing dialect themselves. For example, the tag question [araʔ] was frequently used instead of the standard form *dùi bú dùi* 对不对 'isn't it?'

The teachers also maintained varying attitudes toward the local dialect. All the teachers we observed expressed, at some point, that Putonghua was more beautiful than Nanjinghua. For example, when one teacher at Changjiang Road School presented the syllable jū, a pupil offered a word that sounded like [ʒunu] meaning 'enraged.' The teacher lost her patience and said:

zhè shì nánjīnghuà bùhǎotīng. wǒmen pǔtōnghuà shì
shuō "jīnù".

这是南京话不好听。我们普通话说"激怒"。

'This is Nanjinghua; it sounds awful. In our Putonghua, we say "jīnù"'

Here the teacher identified herself with the Putonghua speech community. At Yizhongxin School this attitude also existed, but it was balanced by expressions of empathy. Wang Mei, when introducing the l-n contrast, explained to the class:

zhè fāyīn duì wǒmen nánjīngrén yǒu kùnnan

这发音对我们南京人有困难

'For we Nanjingers, these sounds are difficult.'

Even as the model Putonghua speaker for the children, she still identified herself as a local person. And as a Nanjinger herself, she too struggled with these sounds.

Summary

Mastering the 63 syllables of Putonghua in a period between five and seven weeks is no easy task. This speed, according to our observations could only be maintained with the help of prior training in Hanyu Pinyin in kindergarten. Even so, the pupils had difficulty with certain sounds and tones. Teachers could predict most of the dialect-based difficulties and so focused extra attention on them. Still, the teachers had to manage 55 children at once. Generally, their approach was continually to model, practice, and revise the sounds with the whole class together. Wang Mei was especially inventive in using games and different techniques to help her pupils. She knew the children were fiercely competitive and so would often have competitions between groups of students as a technique for revising the sounds.

Although both schools had classes of over 50, Changjiang Road School made use of educational technology such as overhead projectors and tape recorders as well as traditional teaching tools. In spite of these advantages, most of the classroom exercises consisted of choral repetition. Yizhongxin School relied only on traditional tools such as chalkboards, slates, and the teacher's techniques. As a result, more games were used, not only to compensate for the lack of technology, but from a realization that these techniques were more efficient for learning than choral repetition.

All the children were expected to memorize the sounds they practiced in class. At the end of the course, each student had to recite the 63 syllables. In addition, they had to learn rules how certain sounds are produced. Many of the rules were in the form of rhymes that were memorized and then chanted by the class. They also were required to know definitions for phonetic terms, for example, *dānyùnmǔ* 单韵母 'monothong' and *fùyùnmǔ* 复韵母 'diphthong.'

Since the vowels were learned first, syllables could be learned as soon as consonants were introduced. Once a syllable was modeled and practiced, then tones were introduced. When a tone was assigned to a syllable, then vocabulary work could begin. It is at this point the teacher worked on sensitizing the pupils to hear the syllable and tone correctly and link them with an acceptable Putonghua vocabulary item. It is also at this stage where the teacher can distinguish between standard and non-standard pronunciation and vocabulary, including those based on local dialects.

The attitude toward local speech was generally negative. At Changjiang Road School, no allowances were given to children who used the Nanjing dialect. At Yizhongxin School, the criticism of the local dialect existed, but it was not as strong. The teacher admitted to the class that many of the difficulties the pupils faced in learning Putonghua were also her own difficulties.

At the completion of the Putonghua and Hanyu Pinyin course, after five to seven weeks, there is a written test. At that time, Putonghua language skills are assessed through reading and writing Hanyu Pinyin. This test we describe in chapter four. The assessment of speaking skills is not done until the end of the semester, after 20 weeks of school. At that time, the skills in Hanyu Pinyin and Chinese characters are also assessed. This final test is described in chapter five.

Chapter Four
Learning Hanyu Pinyin

On the first day of class at Yizhongxin School, four characters were written on the chalkboard in Wang Mei's classroom:

汉语拼音

These Chinese characters stand for Hanyu Pinyin. The task for the next month and a half involved learning the Roman alphabet and reading words transcribed in it, as well as writing words in the alphabet. In spite of the theme of learning the Roman alphabet, the introductory lesson began by presenting the theme, not in Roman letters, but in Chinese characters, again emphasizing the reality of Chinese literacy as literacy in Chinese characters. Wang Mei pointed to the characters and asked the students to repeat after her. The class responded:

hànyǔ pīnyīn

looking at the Chinese characters.

Before any Roman letter is introduced, Wang Mei asked the question: Why do we learn Hanyu Pinyin? Here again it is assumed that the pupils possessed some knowledge about Hanyu Pinyin. We documented the responses that were elicited that day:

kěyǐ rèn zì 可以认字 'can recognize characters'

xúe wàigúo zì 学外国字 'to study foreign characters'

kěyǐ chūgúo 可以出国 'can leave the country'

kàn zì 看字 'to read characters'

yòng zìdiǎn 用字典 'to use the dictionary'

xiě xìn dào shànghǎi he běijīng 写信到上海和北京
'to write a letter to Shanghai and Beijing'

The first response, *kěyǐ rèn zì* 'can recognize Chinese characters' and the response *kàn zì* 'to read characters' indicate an awareness of the educational function of Hanyu Pinyin as a caretaker script in learning Chinese characters. By studying Hanyu Pinyin, one can learn to identify Chinese characters. The *zì* refers to Chinese characters themselves. In addition to the awareness of Hanyu Pinyin's function as a caretaker script, the response *yòng zìdiǎn* 'to use a dictionary' indicates a perception of Hanyu Pinyin as functioning more than a caretaker script, in the sense that it will maintain its utility when consulting reference books. Hanyu Pinyin is useful for looking up a word in standard Putonghua. In most dictionaries, definitions of the word are written in Chinese characters. Hanyu Pinyin can be helpful when looking up a word when the Chinese characters are not recognized by the reader. Dictionaries organize Chinese characters according to numbers of strokes needed for writing them. The characters are also categorized into groups according to character radicals, the root forms. Once the entry is found, the pronunciation of the character can be obtained by reading the Hanyu Pinyin transcription.

The other responses indicate a knowledge of the communicative skills that will be acquired by learning Hanyu Pinyin. The response, *xiě xìn dào shànghǎi he běijīng* 'to write a letter to Shanghai and Beijing,' indicates that even just with Hanyu Pinyin, communication by post is possible. Furthermore, there is an acknowledgement that owing to the widespread use of Putonghua, a letter written in Hanyu Pinyin could be comprehended by readers in both Shanghai and Beijing. At the same time, we have noticed the post office does not always accept domestic letters addressed in Hanyu Pinyin.

Another response indicated that the letters of Hanyu Pinyin possess a similarity to writing systems around the world. The response, *xúe wàiguó zì* 'to study foreign characters' indicates a perception that Hanyu Pinyin, like scripts of many foreign languages, is a Roman alphabet. A knowledge of the Roman alphabet is seen as an asset to learning foreign languages, most likely English. The response *kěyǐ chūguó* 'can leave the country' indicates an understanding of one consequence of having learned a foreign language. Already, the six-year-old knows that for a Chinese person to leave the country, knowledge of a foreign language is necessary. Even at this early age, the child is encouraged to persevere in learning a foreign language to attain what is regarded as a positive prize.

After eliciting the above responses, Wang Mei—using one of her favorite teaching techniques—taught the following rhyme:

pīnyīn zìmǔ yòngchu dà

拼音字母用处大

'the use of the Pinyin alphabet is vast'

dúshū xiězì bìyào de

读书写字必要的

'it is necessary to read and write'

bāng wǒ shuō hǎo pǔtōnghuà

帮我说好普通话

'it helps me speak Putonghua well'

wǒmen juéxīn xué hǎo tā
我们决心学好它
'let's resolve to study it really well'

Although the first line of the rhyme speaks of the multiple functions of Hanyu Pinyin, the rhyme goes on to mention only three. Hanyu Pinyin is useful for (1) reading, (2) writing, and (3) speaking Putonghua. The pupils mentioned the first two functions. But no one mentioned the relationship of Hanyu Pinyin to Putonghua. One pupil did mention that learning the alphabet will provide access to reference material like a dictionary. They will later learn that Hanyu Pinyin is useful in word processing. However, the pupils went beyond the limits of the rhyme and voiced a knowledge of the consequences of learning Hanyu Pinyin. They understood that learning the alphabet may relate to their future foreign language learning. They even understood what rewards success in learning a foreign language could bring.

In the spirit of the first line of the rhyme, "The use of the Pinyin alphabet is vast," William Hannas (1997) suggests a more comprehensive inventory of Hanyu Pinyin functions:

> *Pinyin*'s present formal role as a "notation" belies the fact that it already enjoys de facto status as China's second writing system, with use in Braille, computer inputting, dictionary arrangement, elementary education, foreign language instruction, indexes of all types, international spelling of Chinese words, military communications, minority (non-Han) languages, product brand names and labels, road and railway signs, semaphore, sequencing printed materials, serial designations for machinery and equipment, sign language, standardizing pronunciations, and telegraphy. (p. 25)

We cannot deny that Hanyu Pinyin is used for purposes beyond a caretaker script for learning another script. While these purposes are important, they are not central in the functions of Chinese literacy. Elementary school education reflects this view of Hanyu Pinyin knowledge being useful, and in some cases necessary, but it does not view the alphabet as the principal script for a literate Chinese person.

Shapes of the Alphabet

Learning to read the Roman alphabet is begun the same way as the logographic Chinese characters and that is through pictographs. In the textbook, the letter "b," for example, is likened to a transistor radio. The curved section of the letter is the radio itself and the left-hand tail is a radio antenna sticking up. The "tail" portion of the letter is called a *shǔ* 竖 'vertical line,' the same terminology used for Chinese characters. The shape of a "b" is called a *shǔ he yuán* 竖和圆 'tree and circle.' In the same way, the letter "h" was imposed on a picture of a chair. Every lesson in the textbook begins with an illustration of the letter in which the shape of the letter is compared with a similar looking object. At the Changjiang Road School, the letters were presented on an overhead projector. The mnemonic picture on another transparency was placed over the letter. At Yizhongxin School, the mnemonic devices could be more dramatic. Wang Mei, for example, put a chair on the podium and asked if the chair was like the letter h. The whole class responded:

xiàng 象 'alike.'

When Wang Mei asked the class what the letter o was like, one pupil said it had the shape of a well, that is, a well looking from the top down.

The mnemonic devices were further used in verse. The letter m was learned with the following verse:

liǎngshàn xiǎomen mə-mə-mə

两扇小门 mə-mə-mə

'two small gates mə-mə-mə.'

Verses were also employed to distinguish between difficult visual combinations that appear similar. These difficult combinations included:

i−l, n−m, b−d, t−d, i−j, n−h, p−q, q−g.

To help distinguish between the letters m and n, there is the following verse:

yīshān xiǎomen nə-nə-nə,

liǎngshān xiǎomen mə-mə-mə

一扇小门 nə-nə-nə, 两座小门 mə-mə-mə

'one small gate nə-nə-nə, two small gates mə-mə-mə.'

Illustrations with props were used for these distinctions as well. When contrasting the shape of h with n, the chair on the podium was used to describe h and a stool was used to describe n.

As the lessons continued, the metalanguage of character shapes was increasingly employed. Instead of referring to the mnemonic shapes themselves, the types of strokes necessary for shaping the letters properly were practiced. For example, regarding the shape of the letter b the teacher asked:

zěmeyàng xiě? 怎么样写? 'how do you write it?'

One pupil answered:

shù he yuán 竖和圆 'vertical line and circle.'

While this is correct, the explanation is insufficient in distinguishing the shape of b from that of d. The following two verses explain the shaping of b and d:

zuǒxià bànyuán duo duo duo

左下半圆 哆－哆－哆

'lower right half circle duo-duo-duo'

yòuxià bànyuán bo bo bo

右下半圆 玻－玻－玻

'lower left half circle bo-bo-bo'

In another example, the letter ü is mnemonically depicted in the textbook as a fish's mouth, but the teacher provided a technical explanation of how to write ü:

shù yòu wān shù diǎn diǎn ü-ü-ü

竖右弯竖点点 吁－吁－吁

'vertical line, bend to the right, vertical line, dot dot ü-ü-ü.'

While chanting these verses, the children write the letters in the air with their fingers and then on their desks.

Learning to read and write Hanyu Pinyin begins with the use of visual mnemonic devices. These devices are not dwelt on for long. The metalanguage of character shapes is quickly introduced and pupils are expected to provide a technical explanation of how the shapes are formed. The same process is employed when children learn Chinese characters. Yet with Chinese characters, the mnemonic devices are stronger. This is because in the textbook Chinese characters that are introduced initially, link the user with protoliteracy, that is, the pictographic origins of Chinese characters. In many cases, the relationship between sound and meaning is strong. It is less strong for alphabetical characters because there is no semantic feature attached. For example, the mnemonic device of a transistor radio has nothing to do with the letter b. Radio in Chinese is *shōuyīnjī* 收音机 which does not contain the letter b. However, some mnemonic examples do contain the sound that the letter represents. The selection of *mén* 'gates' for the letter m does include the letter itself and its sound. The same goes for *yǘ* 'fish' for the letter ü.

90

Among the mnemonic devices in the textbook using the shape of the letters, 40% of the example words contain the letters they are describing.

Phonics

At Changjiang Road School, Wang Lan informed us that the method used to teach the sounds and letters is called *zhíhū* 直呼. This method is supposed to be more efficient than the traditional one. According to Wang Lan and Zhu Jialong, as well as Li Jiaqing and Har Jing (1993), the Zhihu method focuses on individual sounds, not syllables. When b is introduced, for instance, the Zhihu method, like conventional phonics methods in English, models the sound as [bə]. The aim is to isolate the consonant sounds and minimize the production of vowel sounds. At Changjiang Road School, for example, a teacher took out a piece of paper to illustrate that the voiceless stops are more aspirated than the voiced. The [pə] sound made the paper move more than the [bə] sound.

The presentation of consonant sounds is done beginning with the bilabials and then working on back to the velars. The traditional method of modeling the sounds is clearly syllabic. In the case of the first consonant sound [b], it is introduced as [buo]. Chinese pupils all across the mainland and Taiwan have learned the consonants as [buo-puo-muo-fuo] and so on. In fact, the non-Roman, Guoyin Zimu alphabet used in pre-1949 Republican China and in Taiwan today is popularily called "bopomofo."

Phonics involves the analysis of the sound and symbol so that the reader can render the pronunciation of a word. Decoding words through their sound analysis (letter phonics) is one approach. Learning to recognize whole words is another. Traditional methods of learning Chinese characters involved a whole-word (or whole-syllable) approach. Chinese characters contain components that are both phonological and semantic. These characters can either stand alone as words or must be bound with other characters to form words. Certain studies in the 1970s experimented with the use of Chinese-type (phonological plus semantic) characters (Rozin, Poritsky, & Sotsky, 1971). Based on their initial success and together with traditions of whole-word methodologies dating back to the eighteenth century such as the "look and say" method (e.g., Mathews, 1966), reading theorists including Frank Smith (1973) began aggressively to advocate a whole-word approach to reading in English. Due to their pictographic origins, Chinese characters appear to lend themselves to whole-word learning. On closer analysis, Chinese characters as pictographic symbols are far removed from the iconic graphs of early Chinese cultures. In fact there is often as much phonological information contained as there is semantic. It has been argued that training children to identify this kind of information in Chinese characters would facilitate their acquisition of more characters (Shu & Anderson, 1997).

In addition, Chinese characters are syllabic. It would, therefore, seem logical that a syllabary, rather than an alphabet, be more appropriate for the Chinese language. In such a system, individual Chinese characters could be selected as representing specific syllables, and words could be constructed from them much like words rendered in Japanese Kana. Syllabaries do have some educational advantages. Syllables can be accurately modeled. With the exception of vowels, sounds represented by alphabets cannot be pronounced in isolation. Many children find difficulty in grasping the abstractness of an alphabet. It has been argued by John Downing (1973) that the relatively high success among Japanese children in their acquisition of literacy lies in the syllabic base of their writing system. Since the Japanese teacher can model a syllable accurately, children can learn the Hiragana and Katakana systems rapidly. Moreover, by providing Japanese reading material with Furigana 'Hiragana alongside of Chinese characters,' the child has access to a great deal more sophisticated texts than an English reader at the same level.

At the same time, not all languages lend themselves to an efficient syllabary. Japanese has a small number of sounds and thus a small number of syllables. In the case of Putonghua, John DeFrancis (1984, p. 42) estimates that there are about 400 syllables in contrast to 113 in Japanese. But if we include the tonal element which is phonemic, the number of syllables can rise to 1277. A syllabary, therefore, for Chinese may not be very efficient.

It has been also suggested that developmental dyslexia is largely absent from children learning to read and write languages that use Chinese characters (e.g., Makita, 1968). This is due to the consistent syllable-grapheme relationship of the Japanese Kana scripts and the semantic nature of Chinese characters. More recent researchers are skeptical. Giovanni B. Flores d'Arcais (1992) suggests that the absence of developmental dyslexia is due more to social factors encouraging children to read, thus promoting compensation strategies for children with the disability. Connie Ho and Peter Bryant (1997) report the existence of special programs in Hong Kong to assist dyslexic children. In the case of adult dyslexia among patients with brain damage, Yin Wengyan and Brian Butterworth (1992) report that their Beijing informants exhibited a similar kind of dyslexia to patients with an alphabetic background. In a study comparing the processing of high frequency and low frequency words in both English and Chinese, M. S. Seidenberg (1985) has found that both English and Chinese readers read high frequency words with minimal reference to the phonetic structure, while both sets of readers employ phonological strategies for low frequency words. In the case of reading aloud, Shengping Fang, Ruey-yun Horng, and Ovid Tzeng (1986) suggest that there is little difference between the cognitive processing of alphabets and Chinese characters.

Since early this century, the choice of phonemic representation of the Chinese language has been an alphabet (as explained in chapter one). While North American teachers may choose between whole-word approaches and phonics analysis approaches as well as eclectic approaches involving both (Durkin, 1993), the official approach in China is phonics analysis. Many of the words are taught using letter phonics, while certain sequences such as nasal endings are taught as cluster phonics as in the following examples:

$$-\text{i an} \quad -\text{in} \quad -\text{i ang} \quad -\text{i ong} \quad -\text{uan}$$

The aim of Zhihu, like other phonics approaches, is to develop the cognitive skills of analysis so that the children can know how a word sounds by the sum of its parts.

In practice, however, the method is not rigidly applied, even though we have observed that it has become more widely adopted. At Changjiang Road School in 1990, almost all the children coming to school with their training at home and kindergarten pronounced their letters as [buo] and [puo] and so on. By 1993, however, we oberved that more children were saying [bə] and [pə]. In fact, one pupil at Yizhongxin School stood up and provided a definition for the Zhihu method. With the pupils already coming to school having learned some letters with Zhihu, teachers like Wang Mei did not go out of their way to emphasize the method. She neither monitored her own modeling of Zhihu carefully nor corrected her pupils' inadvertent "bopomofo's."

Reading Hanyu Pinyin

Even while the shapes of the individual letters were presented and practiced orally, each letter was treated as a syllable, particularly at Yizhongxin School. At Changjiang Road School, there was more of an attempt to be faithful to Zhihu. At both schools, within the first week of Hanyu Pinyin study, the concept of the syllable is introduced. At Yizhongxin School, Wang Mei put the following on the chalkboard:

b−a−> ba

Next she wrote *yīnjié* 'syllable' in Chinese characters:

音节

Wang Mei then explained this word by analyzing the Chinese character components, in spite of the fact that the class had only just begun learning Hanyu Pinyin:

yīnyuède yīn he jiérède jie

音乐的音和节日的节

'the *yīn* for 'music' and the *jie* for 'holiday.''

The class was warned that the lesson was going to be difficult. She followed up this warning by writing a tone mark over the syllable:

bā

mentioning that this meant 'father.' Moreover, the visual representation of tone was presented as a *xiǎomàozi* 小帽子 'little hat.'

To reinforce certain syllables, a game was used. This game, used in both schools, was called: *wǒde péngyou zài nǎli?* 我的朋友在哪里？ 'Where is my friend?' The teacher randomly distributed eight slates around the class. Each slate had a different syllable written on it. Then the teacher selected a slate or flashcard from her own pile, held it up, and called out to the class:

wǒde péngyou zài nǎli?

The pupils looked at their slates to see if they matched the teacher's. If it did, the pupil ran up to the front of the class, held up his or her slate and said,

nǐde péngyou zài zhèlǐ

你的朋友在这里

'your friend is here.'

The pupil then said his or her sound and the whole class repeated it. The game reinforced accuracy in reading syllables. Moreover, the children seemed to enjoy this game.

Another common classroom technique was reading aloud. Teachers paid attention to the correct use of tones, and to rhythm and pace. Most of the reading aloud involved using the textbook, because reading aloud is a skill tested on the semester final examination. Wang Mei mentioned that many children memorized the exercises in the textbook; as a result she wrote her own sentences on the chalkboard, and as the weeks progressed, these sentences became longer. Often the sentences were written on large slates that were propped up on the chalkboard. She began by silently pointing to each word, so the pupils had to read them silently and carefully. Next, she went through the words, saying each one slowly. After this, she asked the class if there were any difficult words. If there were, she wrote these words on the side and would then get the class to sound them out. The next step was to go over the sentences line by line. This would be done by the class as a whole, then by individual rows, and finally by selected pupils. She continually reminded them to read the words correctly, especially the tones. If someone had a problem, Wang Mei would expect the child to sound out the letters. For instance, when the class could not pronounce *tiě* and *chūyi,* she asked them to sound out each letter before finally reading the whole word.

This kind of reading exercise served a number of purposes. It helped train pupils to pay attention to pronunciation, tones, rhythm, and at the same time reviewed different sounds. It also challenged the children as these sentences were not in their textbook, so they were forced to use the skills they had been taught. We did not observe this kind of exercise at Changjiang Road School. Teachers there focused on the textbook. The reading aloud task on the final examination uses a passage from the textbook. In view of this, it is understandable that teachers would concentrate on the textbook. Furthermore, the key school's program was accelerated; therefore there was not a great deal of extra time for teacher-created exercises.

Not all the reading aloud exercises were controlled. In both schools, there were times when the whole class engaged in reading aloud on their own from the textbook. The sound was deafening. These sessions lasted no more than three minutes at a time.

Although most urban children came to school having been introduced to Hanyu Pinyin in kindergarten, school children seemed to have continued difficulty distinguishing between certain sets of the Roman alphabet that have similar shapes. Some of these sets include: b-p-d, q-g, f-t, and m-w. Difficulties persisted even after the introduction to the letters at the beginning of the Hanyu Pinyin course.

Miscuing difficulties did not exist only for syllables with letters from the problematic sets. For example, there was a problem distinguishing t from d. Sometimes tu was pronounced instead of du, or dǎi hu instead of tǎi hu. Part of the difficulty lay in connecting the sounds that the teacher was saying with the points of articulation and the visual letter. The teacher could be pointing to a letter and pronouncing it, but the pupils might be hearing something else. In response to these kinds of difficulties, the overhead transparencies showing points of articulation were an advantage over increased volume in the sound modeling by individual teachers. One solution to distinguishing letters representing similar types and points of articulation is a fill-in exercise. The teacher presented a slate with the following written on it, j (   ) x, and asked what was missing. The answer is the letter q.

There were other kinds of miscues, including ones of a semantic nature. In one sentence, there was the word *xiǎoháizi* 'little child.' The pupil read the sentence saying *xiǎopéngyou* 'little friend.' These two words are obviously synonyms and both would be acceptable in the context. The question remains whether the pupil could not decode *háizi* or instinctively chose *péngyou* as the more felicitous collocation.

Writing Hanyu Pinyin

At both schools, although writing practice was initiated in class, the children usually completed writing exercises for homework. As in the kindergarten, pupils had exercise books in which they practiced writing individual letters and later words and phrases. Some of these exercises appear in the same form on tests. In addition, teachers at both schools often asked pupils to write on the chalkboard and when they did so, teachers asked the class to comment on the writing. They encouraged their pupils to write beautifully. The pupils were harsh critics and offered such opinions like *tàixiǎo* 太小 'too small' or *yǒu máobing* 有毛病 'has a defect.' Despite the possibility of criticism, the children were always eager to be chosen. For example, a group of six pupils went to the chalkboard and wrote the letter a. For most of the letters, the teacher responded *bùcuòde* 不错的 'not bad' but for the letters that were poorly-formed, these were called *cánjirén* 残废人 'disabled persons.' The teachers also received criticism. If they made a mistake in their own chalkboard writing such as placing a wrong tone mark or leaving out punctuation, pupils corrected the teachers who responded by thanking them.

One frequent type of writing exercise was the dictation. The paper used was small, approximately 9 cm by 12 cm. At the top of the paper, the pupils were asked to write, in Hanyu Pinyin, *mòxiě* 默写 'dictation or writing from memory.' Then they wrote their names at the bottom right-hand corner in Chinese characters. Wang Mei was very strict on this formality. The fact that many times the children would not follow this format was a source of great irritation for her. The dictations would include initial and final parts of syllables as well as whole syllables. They would also include actual sentences. In addition, pupils would be asked to produce the 63 initials and finals by heart (See Tables A1 and A2 in the Appendix).

Wang Mei was relatively open about sharing the dictation papers with us. In late September, we detected many difficulties in letter shape formation. By mid-October, many of these difficulties had been overcome. The script difficulties included the letter t being too small and the letters t, f, and j written reversed. Other problems were due to similarity of shape, for example ge for ye.

More of the problems were due to syllable formation and listening accuracy. In Table 9, the errors in the dictation papers that we recorded are listed.

Table 9

Error Analysis of the Dictation Papers

Reversing of order
uw for wu
hz, hc, hs, for zh, ch, sh
ui for iu
iu for ui

Incompletion
w for wu
zh, ch, sh for zhi, chi, shi
z, c, s for zi, ci, si
y for yu
y for yi

98

Coding

wi for wu
ü for yu
zl, cl, sl for zi,ci,si
ie for y
üe, üi, ue, ye, aü for yue

Difficulties in listening accuracy

ne for le
(possible dialect interference)
ri for zhi,chi, shi
zhi, chi, shi for zi,ci,si
(possible hypercorrection, over-compensating for dialect patterns)

Other errors

wu for yu
ri for zi

Not all the writing was controlled in the manner of dictations and writing from memory. Wang Mei, for example, encouraged her pupils to use their knowledge of Hanyu Pinyin and write content of their own choosing. The following is one sample of work written by a pupil after five weeks of Hanyu Pinyin study:

mã ma bã ba lai, wõ ȳi qi qù mãi shū, hõu
lái wõ húi jiā dú shū. 'Mother and father came and together with me went to buy a book, and then went home and I read the book.'

This pupil separated each of the syllables but the spelling and tones are all correct. Not all pupils wrote this well. Others wrote unevenly with poorly formed letters, but in this exercise, they were writing on their own.

Hanyu Pinyin and Chinese Morphology

Whether or not to write Hanyu Pinyin as separate individual syllables is an issue of Chinese morphology. All Chinese characters look individual, so it would seem that the romanized equivalent should also look the same way. On a closer examination, individual Chinese characters do not possess the same utility in a sentence. Most are content words and usually form parts of word compounds. Others are function words, providing grammatical meaning (Y. Hu, 1962). Among the characters that possess grammatical functions, some tend toward free forms while others tend toward being bound as affixes.

The nineteenth century German philologist Wilhelm von Humboldt classified the languages of the world into three groups: isolating, agglutinating, and inflecting. His classification, based on morphology, grouped languages together in terms of how words were formed (Robins, 1988). He called Chinese an isolating language because each morpheme (or each syllable) could serve as an independent word. In a Wenyan text particularly, each character does tend to stand for a separate word. That is one reason why it differed so much from spoken Chinese. Agglutinating languages, like Japanese, tend to form words by adding strings of affixes. In many Indo-European languages, the tendency is to inflect, creating words by changing their internal make-up such as the conjugation of French verbs.

Language typologies of this kind oversimplify linguistic realities. English does agglutinate with many suffixes and Chinese also can have multi-syllable words. Most words today in Putonghua consist of two or more syllables. T. J. Huang and I. M. Liu (1978) have found that from a word list of 40,032 words, 65.15% of them are two-syllable words. The textual layout of a Chinese-character text looks superficially as though it consists of isolated words. Only the literate can predict where the word boundaries are.

The layout of the Chinese characters has powerfully influenced the way Hanyu Pinyin is represented. In the conventions of a Chinese-character text, it is not necessary to indicate word boundaries, but in the case of Hanyu Pinyin, most recent dictionaries that employ Hanyu Pinyin provide entries as words not as separate syllables (e.g., J. Wu, 1985). Although many of the content morphemes forming compound words are relatively easy to pick out and write as single words, a problem arises for function morphemes—whether or not to attatch them to the preceeding (or in some cases, the following) word. Some function morphemes appear to be stable and are consistently bound to the preceeding words. Two of these examples include the aspect particles, *le* 了 and *guo* 过. Some of the more unstable function morphemes include *bu* 不 'negative' and three different kinds of *de*, as 的 'modifier,' 地 'adverbial adjunct,' and 得 'verbal complement marker.' These sometimes appear bound to words or as free forms.

Paul L. King (1983) conducted an experiment where native speakers of Chinese were asked to parse a continuous text into words. He found that especially for *de*, the tendency was to bind it to the preceeding word if it was a single syllable. If the preceeding word had two or more syllables, then the particle stood as a free form. King concluded that two syllables are seen to be an appropriate length of a word in Chinese if there is a choice. Two-syllable words are not the only possibilities based on textual sensibilities. Four-syllable words have traditionally existed in the form of slogans and proverbs, as well as restaurant menu items.

Various approaches to word formation can be seen in the use of Hanyu Pinyin in captions and billboards. The Chinese Railroads is one context where Hanyu Pinyin is used a great deal. On the platforms, the names of the stations are written in isolating syllables. For example:

延　安
YAN　AN

On the destination boards on the carriages, the place names are written as a single word:

延安
YANAN

A street sign in Chongqing employed another strategy by indicating word boundaries:

筷子　街

Kuaizi Jie
'chopstick street'

Zhu Jialong of the Jiangsu Province Education Commission asserted that the aim of Hanyu Pinyin education, among other goals, is to encourage a sense of word formation. Yet we did not observe this being taught at either school. In the textbooks and on the chalkboard, sentences were written in isolated syllables or written together in one long word. However, often bi-syllable and multi-syllable words were written on slates as single words. In the context of sentences or longer texts, no word boundaries were indicated. The textbook also presented text in isolating syllables. When we questioned Wang Mei about this, her response was that keeping the syllables separate was a preparation for learning Chinese characters. The lack of training in identifying real lexical boundaries, and the lack of such boundaries in the use of Hanyu Pinyin in school materials reinforce the caretaker status of Hanyu Pinyin in the first-grade curriculum.

Hanyu Pinyin and English

In the course of our observation, we learned about the teaching of English to children. English instruction is not part of the elementary school curriculum in Nanjing until the fifth grade. At the same time, however, English instruction to children is not an entirely new idea. In 1971, there was an experiment in Shanghai where three elementary schools introduced English in grade one. The children were taught to listen and speak, but not to read as the teachers did not want to cause any confusion between the romanized system as used in Hanyu Pinyin and in English ("Some Experiences," 1972/1976). Today, the instruction often occurs in private classes in homes or in private schools, as well as in some enterprising kindergartens.

At the Nanjing University Kindergarten, where we observed children learning Hanyu Pinyin, English instruction was not offered. However, several children, presumably children of academics, were learning English and this was immediately evident from their knowledge of upper-case letters. The Hanyu Pinyin used in schools to learn to read Chinese does not include upper-case letters.

A knowledge of English romanization may be a predictable phenomenon in an academic community. Indeed we had colleagues, who with their English-proficient spouses, endeavored to raise their child bilingually in English and Chinese. But our attention to the issue of alphabetic biliteracy was drawn not by what we observed at the Nanjing University Kindergarten, but at Yizhongxin School where most of the children did not come from homes of intellectuals. When Wang Mei asked how many first graders were learning English, 14 raised their hands. Her attitude was positive. She said:

yībiān xué hànyǔ pīnyīn, yībiān xué yīngyǔ, hěn
yǒnggǎn

一边学汉语拼音，一边学英语，很勇敢

'On the one hand you study Hanyu Pinyin and on the other you study English.
You are courageous.'

In urban schools, like Yizhongxin School, there is an understanding that proficiency in English is an asset in today's world. The economic liberalization since the late 1970s has emphasized the view that contact with the outside world brings opportunity and money. There are English language learning programs on radio and TV that are popular with a wide range of listeners from elementary pupils to research scientists (Lu, 1991; Zhan, 1990). Notwithstanding the relationship of English to the future career opportunities for children, English continues to remain an important academic subject in secondary and tertiary institutions. By starting to learn English at an early age, success in the competition for access to these institutions is seen to be strengthened. Moreover, English classes, like piano, violin, or dancing classes, constitute part of the extracurricular cultural training that many urban parents are intent on offering their only child.

Because we did not observe any early childhood classes in English, we have not documented difficulties children encountered related to the interference of Hanyu Pinyin on their English learning. We have observed, however, that many children do know the English pronunciation of the letters. For example, the letter z was pronounced as [zi:] in the American way. Many children seemed to know the alphabet song with the American pronunciation. Some schools teach the alphabet song with the Hanyu Pinyin pronunciation. Although we never heard this song sung at the schools we observed, children we know reported that the song was sung as follows:

a-bo-ce-do-e-fo-ge, and so on.

At school many children knew the numbers, as well as greetings in English. When we would arrive in the classroom, a lot of children would rush over to us and say "hello," and shake our hands. When we left, many would say "good-bye." Once when the teacher was presenting the syllable *lóu* and elicited vocabulary examples from the children, one child said:

'hello' de lóu.

The teacher accepted this English example for a Chinese syllable. Another example where an English option was accepted is when the letter k was presented. One child offered "OK" as an example. It could be argued that "OK" is already a word in Chinese, used as part of the loan word from Japanese: 卡拉 OK 'karaoke.' In a further example when the syllable *tí* was presented, one child offered:

'do-re-mi-fa-so-la-ti-do' de tī.

In contrast to vocabulary examples offered in the local Nanjing dialect, the English examples were always acceptable and even praised. This could be a consequence of either our presence in the classroom or the reality that English is a part of the required school curriculum in the higher grades.

More study is needed to document the relationship of Hanyu Pinyin to the learning of English. Further study is also needed to ascertain whether early childhood English education does indeed interfere with the learning of Hanyu Pinyin as the Shanghai schools in the early 1970s feared. Our study suggests that such interference is minimal. Instead, it appears that English is yet another component to the Chinese child's total literacy acquisition process.

Testing Hanyu Pinyin

After six and a half weeks of Hanyu Pinyin instruction (five weeks at Changjiang Road School), a test is given to assess the extent to which the children have learned Hanyu Pinyin. We received test papers from both schools. We also received test papers for the mid-term, administered in early November, and the final examination, administered in mid-January. The final examination was the same for both schools. Because the latter two tests measure ability in both Hanyu Pinyin and Chinese characters, they will be discussed in chapter five.

The nature of all three tests further emphasizes Hanyu Pinyin's caretaker status. The tests for only Hanyu Pinyin are, at least in Nanjing, teacher- (or school) prepared tests. Although the mid-term tests are also prepared by the teacher or school, they shared more similarities than the Hanyu Pinyin tests. The final tests, published in Beijing, represent a nation-wide administration. Generally, in education, the assessment of material that is left up to individual teachers or schools is seen as less important than the material assessed on tests prepared for wider use. It follows that the use of Hanyu Pinyin in conjunction with Chinese characters is more important than the use of Hanyu Pinyin by itself.

The Hanyu Pinyin test papers prepared by each of the schools we observed, however, are significant for our study. They share similar kinds of items and have most of the directions written in Chinese characters. Their differences lie in the kinds of Hanyu Pinyin knowledge skills required. In Table 10, a comparison of the Hanyu Pinyin tests prepared by each school is presented.

Table 10
The Hanyu Pinyin Test

Changjiang Road School	Yizhongxin School
Part 1 11% Copy the six vowels: u i o a e ü.	Part 1 23% Dictation of 20 syllable-initial sounds.

Part 2 18% Find the initial sounds in 12 syllables and write them in the parentheses. e.g., mǎ (m)	Part 2 13.5% Copy nine syllable finals. e.g., ang
Part 3 19% Ten pictures of animals are provided. Write the name of each animal in the parentheses below each picture. (The names of the ten animals are provided, thus the task involves matching and copying)	Part 3 22% Write syllables from the 22 sets of letters provided (ten sets contain "ü"). e.g., j-i-> ji j-üe-> jue
Part 4 22% Copy the initial letters of the following ten syllables: qiāo yuán dǐng xī māo rì huī yīn shǔ yuè	Part 4 5% Write the missing part of the following five syllables (No directions are provided, only the following example). e.g., bō -> b - (ō)
Part 5 23% Select the correct pronunciation for the following eight pictures. e.g., peach soap light bulb cor.: táo zi féi zào diàn dēng inc.: táo zī féi zhào dàn dēng	Part 5 24% Write the word for the following eight pictures. e.g., umbrella yǔ sǎn
Part 6 7% There are four sentences below. Underline the syllables that contain a tone. e.g., yàn zi fēi huí lái le.	Part 6 6.5% Look at the picture and write a sentence.
	Part 7 6% Read the following rhyme and write the letter it refers to.

Comparing these two tests, the test prepared at Yizhongxin School is more demanding than the one made by Changjiang Road School. For example, there is a dictation section which does not appear in Changjiang Road School's test. In addition, there are more productive skills demanded on Yizhongxin School's test. Together with the dictation section, the pupils must, in response to pictures, produce two-syllable words. Furthermore, they are asked to write a full sentence. In contrast, Changjiang Road School's test only demanded production of single-syllable words to pictures and even provided an answer list for pupils to select from. The other section with pictures simply demanded a choice from two options. It is curious that the key school should prepare a less demanding test than the neighborhood school. However, upon analysis of both tests, we found them both faithful to the materials that each school emphasized in class. From that perspective, these tests served the purpose of achievement tests. For example, Wang Mei spent a considerable amount of time teaching the use of ü. Almost an entire section on the test was devoted to this letter. In addition, dictation and rhymes to remember pronunciation and letter formation were used throughout the weeks. These items also appeared on the test. In contrast, the Changjiang Road School test emphasized Putonghua vis-a-vis local dialect. This was done by making the distracters on the picture identification item represent problems of interference with regional speech patterns.

Two of the three examples presented above explain this:

e.g.,	peach	soap	lightbulb
correct:	tǎo zi	féi zào	diǎn dēng
incorrect:	tǎo zǐ	féi zhào	dàn dēng

The pronunciation of "peach" tested the correct use of tone. For "soap," the contrast between z and zh was focused on. Generally, Putonghua speakers of Southern Mandarin and Wu have a tendency to pronounce words with /zh/ using /z/ (explained in chapter three). Because of this tendency, there may be a pattern to hypercorrect or over-generalize, that is, pronounce all words with z as zh. In this test item, the word with z is the correct one, thus checking for any hypercorrection. In the third example, the Nanjing dialect is focused on. As mentioned in chapters one and three, there is a tendency in Nanjing speech to pronounce the diphthongs in Putonghua as monothongs. Therefore *diǎn* would be pronounced as *dàn*. In contrast, the Yizhongxin School test did not focus on dialect. For the same kind of item on the test, the pupils had to write in their own words. Various orthographic difficulties could be predicted, in addition to dialect-based pronunciation difficulties.

We were unable to obtain test scores at Changjiang Road School.

However, at Yizhongxin School, Wang Mei showed us the test scores from her class. All the pupils, except for two, scored over 80%. Most scored over 90%. The two who scored lower than 80% scored in the low 60s. These results were gained in spite of the rigorous nature of the test.

Summary

The study of Hanyu Pinyin began with learning the shapes. Although mnemonic devices were used to help remember the shapes, the metalanguage of character shapes and strokes was quickly introduced and pupils were expected to describe the shape of a letter correctly.

When reading and writing Hanyu Pinyin, some children had perceptual difficulties with similarly shaped letters like d and b. Others had difficulties in forming syllables. In dictation exercises, some had difficulty distinguishing between sounds that had similar places of articulation. Others had difficulty distinguishing between sounds that have similar manner of articulation. When the pupils wrote their own Hanyu Pinyin sentences, each syllable was isolated. Although some syllables combine naturally as words, this was not corrected because word boundaries are not explicitly indicated in texts written in Chinese characters.

The assessment of Hanyu Pinyin was done by tests created in each school. The tests reflected the relative emphases of the schools. In the test given by Changjiang Road School, proper pronunciation of words in Putonghua was stressed. At Yizhongxin School, dictation and writing of Hanyu Pinyin was emphasized.

The ability to read and write in Hanyu Pinyin and thus become literate so much more quickly and easily than in Chinese characters was cited as an important reason for learning Hanyu Pinyin in an essay by Wu Yuzhang, Chairman of the Committee for Chinese Writing Reform. The essay was originally published soon after elementary schools began using Hanyu Pinyin.

At New Year's time I received a few letters from first-year primary school students. They had been studying less than half a year; they still could not write letters in Chinese characters so they used the phonetic alphabet. They wrote what they themselves wanted to say, and their writing was not at all stilted. (1959/1979, p. 301-302)

Wang Mei's pupils were encouraged to use their new skills and, as the example illustrates, they were able to communicate their thoughts effectively. Within a few weeks, the pupils would have to shift to learning to read and write characters, a much more prolonged process.

Chapter Five

Learning Chinese Characters

In mid-October after the lessons in Hanyu Pinyin were completed, the children began lessons in learning Chinese characters. The mood was less spirited than when the Hanyu Pinyin lessons started in early September. There was no eliciting from the children of reasons why learning Chinese characters was a good idea. Instead, the classes plunged directly into the task. At Yizhongxin School, Wang Mei began the new subject with a solemn announcement:

wǒmén shì zhōngguórén. zhōngguó de wénzì bùhé qítā
guójiā de wénzì yīyàng.

我们是中国人。中国的文字不和其他国家的文字一样。

'We are Chinese. Chinese writing is not the same as the writing of other countries.'

Thus, pupils learn to read and write not only for practical purposes: They do so to participate in a coming-of-age ritual that possesses national significance. By learning the writing system, one enters a 3000-year-old tradition. This literacy experience will reinforce both cultural and national identities. Some people fear that the persisting problem of illiteracy endangers the continuity of Chinese culture ("Efforts Made," 1991). Consequently, by becoming literate in Chinese characters, the transfer of the cultural tradition is maintained.

The linguistic definition of Chinese characters has been an issue of debate. Popularly, they have been defined as "pictographic," "ideographic," or "logographic." The problem with these terms is not that they are incorrect, but that they fail to encompass the scope of the kinds of characters in use. More precise definitions include "morphographic" (DeFrancis, 1984) or "morpheme-syllable" (Coulmas, 1989). These definitions focus on the fact that each Chinese character does stand for a morpheme, a meaning unit, but not necessarily for a full word. Florian Coulmas's definition further includes the phonetic nature of Chinese characters, in that they stand for a syllable rather than a single sound. These two aspects set the Chinese writing system apart from alphabets. However, rather than use these definitions as a metalanguage of the writing system, we will continue, as John DeFrancis suggests, simply to refer to them as "Chinese characters."

To become functional with Chinese characters, a knowledge of between 4000 (Hannas, 1997) and 6000 (Li & Har, 1993) characters is needed. This is the target for acquisition in the nine years of compulsory education. By the end of elementary school, children are expected to know between 2500 (Lewin, Xu, Little, & Zheng, 1994), 2834 (Taylor & Taylor, 1995), and 3500 characters (Zhu Jialong, personal communication, 1990). Although all our sources claim to use official numbers, we see that there is a great deal of variation. The number of Chinese characters necessary to perform certain functions can only be estimated. Media reports of government literacy campaigns describe varying levels of literacy. Those defined as "literate" in urban areas must be able to read 2000 characters, while in the rural areas they must read 1500 characters ("Blueprint for 20m," 1992).

It is relatively well-known that even with the smaller estimates, the task of learning so many characters is one of great magnitude. What is less known is the kind of surprise that Chinese children experience when they first encounter a Chinese character lesson in school.

The Chinese Character Lesson

From the beginning of Hanyu Pinyin training, as soon as syllables are introduced, the teacher elicits vocabulary containing that particular syllable. When a syllable marked with one of the four tone diacritics is presented, pupils realize that the range of possibilities for that particular syllable shrinks. Any vocabulary item containing the correct sound and tone was acceptable. However, when Chinese characters are introduced, far fewer words are acceptable because the words must contain not only the correct sound, but also be written with the correct character.

The first character introduced was the character " 一 " *yī* 'one.' The teacher asked the pupils how it was written:

yīzi zěnmeyàng xiě?　"一" 字怎么样写?

The children answered:

héng héng héng yī yī yī　横 横 横 一 一 一
'to the side, side, side, yi-yi-yi.'

Then the teacher elicited vocabulary with the character " 一 ." One child said:

yī jià fēijī 一架飞机 'one airplane.'

Another child said:

yīkuài qù 一块去 'let's go together.'

A third child said:

yīfu de yī 衣服的 " 一 " 'the yī of clothes.'

The teacher refused this last example. Up until now vocabulary like this had been acceptable, but now with Chinese characters, further semantic distinctions must be exercised. Both " 衣 " and " 一 " have the same sound and tone, but they have different meanings. The distinctions between them are represented by different symbols in the script.

Not all the children in the class began studying Chinese characters with the same background knowledge. The degree to which the children had been introduced to Chinese characters before grade one seemed to depend on the home environment. At the Nanjing University Kindergarten, we observed a child who could read, in Chinese characters, the names of all his classmates. This kind of prodigious ability is often reported in the media. There are private programs in urban areas to train these child prodigies, indicating parental enthusiasm for early learning. For example, a program developed by Fang Dequan teaches Chinese characters to toddlers and by the time they reach three or four years old, some children can recognize over 2000 characters ("Talented Tots," 1992). A child prodigy is defined in terms of the number of characters the child knows.

Before children begin school, between August 16 and 22, there is an orientation week for first graders. We were informed that most parents teach their children to write their names in Chinese characters, but if children come to school without this basic skill, the teachers will teach them how to write their names during the first week.

On the first day when Chinese character lessons began, one teacher announced a well-known maxim in literacy:

xiě duì he xiě hǎo kàn

写对和写好看

'write correctly and write beautifully.'

To engage in this task, the pupils must pay attention to two aspects of writing Chinese characters: type of stroke and stroke order. Like learning the shapes of the Roman alphabet, learning the names of the various kinds of strokes is done with rhymes and chants. For the character " 三 " *sān* 'three' the teacher asked the following:

sān de zì zěnmeyàng xiě?

"三" 字怎么样写?

'How do you write the character, "三" ?'

The class responded with the following rhyme:

sān héngxiàn sān sān sān
三横线, 三, 三, 三
'Three horizontal lines sān sān sān.'

To form the character "二," the teacher explained in this way:

duǎn yīdiǎn he cháng yīdiǎn
短一点和长一点
'Short a little and long a little.'

Then each pupil, with his or her index finger, traced the shape of the character in the air. After that, they practiced drawing the shape with their fingers on the desks. For a character with multiple kinds of strokes, like "六" 'number six,' the following instruction was given:

liù de zì diǎn héng piě diǎn
六的字点横撇点
'For the number six, dot, horizontal line, left-falling stroke, dot.'

The sequence of strokes is extremely important. The characters cannot be shaped correctly unless the strokes are written in the correct order. This becomes increasingly important in the writing and decoding of cursive forms. The textbook and published workbooks number the strokes for each Chinese character that they introduce. Once the basic characters are presented, only the additional strokes are numbered.

The children practice writing Chinese characters in notebooks with printed squares rather than lines. These squares are called *tiánzìgé* 填字格. In each square, there is a horizontal and vertical dotted line, creating a cross. The task for the learner is to write the character in the square with the correct proportions. In our observations, we have noticed that characters with more vertical lines seemed initially easier for the children. Characters with horizontal lines like 二 were more problematic to reproduce because of the difficulty of gauging the middle ground above and below the horizontal axis. The top line of character 二 is in the upper two quadrants while the bottom line is in the lower two quadrants. For the character 六, the horizontal line is written just above the central axis. If that position can be anchored correctly, the rest of the strokes can be easily written in a proportional manner.

At the initial stages of learning Chinese characters, the relationship of the modern forms to their pictographic origins is highlighted. The textbooks introduce Chinese characters, like they do for the alphabet, with visual mnemonic devices. For Chinese characters, this process takes on more significance because of their semantic component. For example, the character for mountain 山 (*shān*) is superimposed on a mountain with three peaks. The character for paddy field 田 (*tián*) is superimposed on four square rice paddies, and so on.

However, despite the origins of Chinese characters, characters with distinct iconic values are actually few in number. The textbook tends to group these together. Most Chinese characters have lost their iconic values, and since the Qin standardization over 2000 years ago, they have become largely symbolic. Moreover, the information provided by the characters tends to contain as much phonetic information as semantic (DeFrancis, 1984; 1989). In Putonghua, Chinese characters with similar shapes tend to share phonological similarities. However, this pattern is not exploited in the first-grade textbooks.

Often the transition of pictographic writing systems from a semantic to a phonological base involves the development of rebuses. A rebus is a symbol with a phonological value to it. Among the partially literate in China, there is a tendency to use certain Chinese characters for their phonological value, not for the semantic value in standard usage. Several private restaurant entrepreneurs in Nanjing advertised their alcoholic beverages with signs bearing the following character:

汍 jiū

The standard form is:

酒　jiǔ

Both 九 'nine' and 酒 'alcoholic beverage' have the same pronunciation and tone. The water radical 氵 is attached to the more basic number nine character to indicate a kind of liquid. Because it sounds the same as 'alcohol,' it was chosen over the more complicated standard form. In this case, the meaning of 'nine' ceases to exist—only its pronunciation remains. This kind of non-standard use of Chinese characters is widespread. Between 1989 and 1990, the Beijing Language Commission found more than 27,000 cases of non-standard characters used on signs in the capital (Xi, 1991). In the schools, there is an attempt to teach the standard forms. How much of school literacy is retained in adulthood is a matter for further research.

In chapter three we summarized the Putonghua lesson involving learning Hanyu Pinyin and standard pronunciation and vocabulary. In Table 11, the initial lessons learning Chinese characters are summarized.

Table 11

The Initial Lessons Learning Chinese Characters

1. The characters to be learned are written on the chalkboard.
2. The teacher demonstrates how the character is written paying attention to the type of strokes and the order of strokes.
3. For a representative character, the class will learn a rhyme describing stroke type and order.
4. The teacher elicits vocabulary that uses the character.
5. After all the characters have been introduced, pupils practice writing the characters in workbooks with tianzige.
6. Using the textbook the class practices reading aloud.

The Textbook

There is a popular impression that learning Chinese characters is mostly a calligraphic exercise with rote learning (e.g., Gerbault, 1997). Certainly calligraphy with charcoal ink and brush is a component of Chinese character

116

learning that exists across China, Korea, and Japan. Repeated practice and rote learning, we have also observed, constitute a part of the learning process. There is some question as to how much practice is necessary. For example, parents have criticized the necessity of copying a character eight times when twice was seen as enough ("Homework to be Cut," 1992).

Repeated practice, however, is not the whole task of acquisition. Although we were able to observe only one week of Chinese character instruction at both schools, we noticed that as soon as the shapes of the characters were introduced, the class engaged in vocabulary work, primarily working with the pupils' background knowledge. Thus the instruction was quickly applied to the children's own world.

The textbook for the first semester of first grade (*Yuwen*, 1990) does not arrange the Chinese characters according to stroke complexity. In other words, the material is not arranged strictly according to difficulty. The first set of characters presented are the numbers one through ten. Notice that number five has four strokes and number four has five:

一　　二　　三　　四　　五　　六　　七　　八　　九　　十

'One,' 'two,' and 'three' may be iconic, but the rest are symbolic, their shape having no connection to their intrinsic meaning. The presentation of the characters in the textbook is arranged according to topics and semantic fields. After the numbers one through ten are presented, the following "iconic" set is introduced:

日　　月　　水　　火　　山　　石　　田　　土　　方
'sun'　'moon' 'water' 'fire' 'mountain' 'stone' 'paddy' 'soil' 'direction'

This set relates to the natural world, except no picture was provided for 方 'direction.'

The next chapter provides the following set in order to read about the human body:

人　耳　目　手　足　上　　中　　下　　大　　小　　了
'person' 'ear' 'eye' 'hand' 'foot' 'above' 'middle' 'below' 'large' 'small' 'completion'

Two lessons further the following set appears:

东　西　南　北　左　右　马　牛　羊　儿　在　青
'east' 'west' 'south' 'north' 'left' 'right' 'horse' 'cow' 'sheep' 'child' 'at' 'green'

Notice that the sets get longer—the more one knows, the more one can learn. Moreover, notice the range of complexity. For example, 南 'south' and 青 'green' are more complex than, say, 牛 'cow' or 儿 'child.' Yet both 南 and 青 are made up of components, such as 羊, 土, and 月, that are being and have been learned. That is why increasing the number of characters to be learned is not seen as an inordinate burden.

Other traditional methods involve presenting Chinese characters in groups of similar shapes rather than by themes. According to Evelyn Rawski's (1979) sources, many of the school textbooks in the Qing dynasty period also organized characters in meaningful groups similar to the way it is done today. Illustrated glossaries were used extensively and they helped overcome the problem of varying speech varieties. Square wooden blocks with characters carved on them were also used for learning. These blocks could be shuffled like a deck of cards and thus be used to check if students had memorized the characters.

Based on experiments conducted in Heilongjiang Province in the early 1980s, elementary schools in China today actively promote the use of the intertext stage, that is, using texts with both Hanyu Pinyin and Chinese characters (Dai & Lu, 1985; Hawkins & Stites, 1991). This method is seen to motivate children as they can engage in communicative writing early on. As they learn more Chinese characters, gradually they use less and less Hanyu Pinyin.

Unlike in the People's Republic and Taiwan, in Hong Kong alphabets are not used for learning Chinese characters. Beginning at the age of three, characters are learned as whole words. Connie Ho and Peter Bryant (1997) have found that without having been taught, children spontaneously employ rules for detecting phonological cues in Chinese characters. In their study in a Beijing elementary school, Hua Shu and Richard Anderson (1997) report that first graders are not taught skills of morphological analysis, particularly with radicals, that may help them predict the sound and meaning of unfamiliar characters. Because we were unable to observe further Chinese character-learning classes, we are not in a position to dispute this. We can only say that based on the Hanyu Pinyin instruction which offered morphological analysis, we would predict that the same effort would be made when radicals are introduced.

In addition to the character and vocabulary presentation in the textbook, each lesson has a full-page picture. There are more pictures in an experimental series of textbooks (not used in either school) called *Shuohua* 说话。The task involves talking about what is going on in the picture. Already on the Hanyu Pinyin test, pupils were required to write a sentence about a picture's content. In the textbook, as well as on the tests, pupils are expected to practice and demonstrate their oral skills. If textbook pictures are used for speaking practice and even classroom discussions, then what sort of images and content do the pictures depict?

In the 1990s, the society of China represented in elementary school textbooks is a world in which most people live in an urban area (Allen & Ingulsrud, 1998). It is a colorful world where children are surrounded by trees, flowers, family, and friends. At home, children usually have their own room with a desk and toys. The homes are comfortable and well-furnished while modern appliances such as a TV and refrigerator are common. Parents, grandparents, and pets are all part of the family unit. Food is plentiful and everyone is well-dressed. Children are encouraged to work hard, help others, and respect their elders. The older children make sure the younger ones obey rules such as not picking flowers in the parks, dropping litter, or being selfish. Children are usually with others either in school or the playground. When they are by themselves such as at home, then they are quiet and productive. They either do their homework or relax with a puzzle. If they are girls, they help with the housework. In all the textbooks, the illustrations suggest ideas about what the boys and girls might like to be. There appear to be signals about appropriate goals.

While men and boys seem to lead more active lives, the career choices emphasize the military and agriculture. Despite the changes since the opening up of the economy in the late 1970's, there are no clear illustrations of modern jobs showing men working with computers or in private enterprise. On the other hand, there are a number of pictures of men in suits carrying briefcases, so perhaps they may be considered business men or officials although it is not clear what type of business is involved.

The message for girls is more explicit. Women are always busy with housework and their job. Girls are their main helpers and are thus trained from the beginning of elementary school to think about their future dual role of working outside the home and being responsible for the family (Croll, 1995; Honig & Hershatter, 1988; Wolf, 1985). The main career for women is teaching, particularly being an elementary school teacher. Glamorous careers such as being a model, singer, or movie star are unrepresented even though they currently have wide appeal in the media (Croll, 1995).

Testing Chinese Literacy Skills

Whereas both the Hanyu Pinyin test and the mid-term test were prepared by the individual schools, the final test for the semester was published in Beijing by Renmin Jiaoyu Chubanshe（人民教育出版社）and used in both schools. The Hanyu Pinyin test administered in each school differed on a number of points reflecting the relative emphases of the teachers. Although the mid-term test was similar, for example, both tests required pupils to write the 23 initial sounds from memory, there were two important differences. First, there was the quality of duplication. The Changjiang Road School test had a better format and the print was much clearer. Second, Changjiang Road School had an accelerated program, compressing six years of elementary school into five. Their Hanyu Pinyin instruction lasted five weeks in contrast to the six and a half weeks at Yizhongxin School. Therefore, their mid-term test had more items on Chinese characters than the Yizhongxin School test. Still, the semester final test was the same for both the five-year and six-year school. In chapter four we described the school-based tests; here we will describe the test published by Renmin Jiaoyu Chubanshe and administered across Nanjing.

The test in Chinese language, administered in late January measures the literacy skills of children after four and a half months in school. There are two sections: a written section and an oral section. The content of the test beginning with the written section is analyzed in Table 12.

Table 12
Yuwen First Semester Final Examination (written section)

Part 1   8 marks

Write the initial letter of each syllable in the parentheses below: e.g., f ē i （ f ）

Part 2   6 marks

Select the syllables from the following list and write them below:

bǐ u jǐn wǔ zh wéi ü yuè zh mō

correct: bǐ jǐn wǔ wéi yuè mō

Part 3   12 marks

Look at the six pictures, read the Hanyu Pinyin, and write Chinese characters for each: e.g.,   picture of calligraphy brush

máo   bǐ

（ 毛 ）   （ 笔 ）

Part 4   12 marks

Read the Hanyu Pinyin and write Chinese characters (twelve characters):

e.g.,   zhōng   guó

（ 中 ）   （ 国 ）

Part 5   12 marks

Write two Chinese characters for each of the six radicals below:

e.g.,   女 妈 好

Part 6   9 marks

Write the word in Chinese characters for each of the six pictures below:

　　　　　e.g.,　　　　picture of stars

　　　　　　　　（　　星星　　）

Part 7   12 marks

Using the following six Chinese characters, create words (with other characters):

　　　　　e.g.,　　　民（　人民　）

Part 8   15 marks

Read the Hanyu Pinyin and write three sentences (in Chinese characters):

　　　　　e.g.,　qiū　　tiān　　dào　　le

　　　　　　（ 秋 ）　（ 天 ）　（ 到 ）　（ 了 ）。

Part 9   8 marks

Look at the four pictures and complete the sentences below (in Chinese characters):

　　　　　e.g.,　picture of boy reading a book

　　　　　　他在（ 看 ）（ 书 ）。

Part 10   6 marks

Copy the following Chinese characters in the *tiānzìgé* boxes below:

　　水　　还　　做　　走　　要　　很

122

Part 11   10 marks
Look at the picture and write three sentences:
  Picture of a little girl walking to school with the sun shining and a
  bird singing.
  Criteria: Give three points for the first two sentences and four points for the
  third. For a very creative sentence, give five points.

The scores for this test add up to 110. The directions for each part are written in both Hanyu Pinyin and Chinese characters. In contrast, for the school-made tests at both schools, including the Hanyu Pinyin tests, all directions were in Chinese characters.

By the end of the first semester, the focus is clearly on Chinese characters. Although knowledge of Hanyu Pinyin is needed for 5 of the 11 parts, the kind of knowledge required is receptive. No part required the productive skills of Hanyu Pinyin without any visual clues.

The material is tested in order of difficulty. The first two parts test syllable structure through Hanyu Pinyin. Chinese characters are tested from part 3 on. In part 3, there is both a picture and a Hanyu Pinyin prompt. In part 4, there is only a Hanyu Pinyin prompt. From part 8 on, except for part 10, there is a deliberate attempt to measure Chinese character use in the context of a sentence. In part 11, in particular, there is an open-ended task where pupils write their own sentences. Only part 10 tests calligraphic skills and it constitutes just six marks. Although teachers encourage students to write beautifully, it is clear from the test that demonstration of skill in calligraphy is less important than the ability to use Chinese characters in context.

In addition to the written test, there is a speaking section in which teachers have individual interviews with all the students. The aim of the test is to measure Putonghua speaking skills. There are two parts, reading aloud and speaking. The first part involves reading a short passage from the textbook. The passage is about 60 syllables long and it is written, not in Chinese characters, but in Hanyu Pinyin.

The second part involves talking about a series of three pictures. In the test paper we received, there is a story based on an old man walking through the snow. Two school children assist the old man and deliver him safely to his door. Test items employing series of pictures also occur in English proficiency tests. The Test of Spoken English (TSE) published by Educational Testing Service, for example, contains a similar kind of item to provide material for measuring speaking ability.

Together with the sample final examination are the criteria for assessing spoken skills. In Table 13, the criteria in Chinese with an English translation are provided:

Table 13

Criteria for Yuwen First Semester Final Examination (Speaking Section)

Criteria for Reading Aloud

优: 能用普通话读。不丢字，不添字，不指读，读的正确，流利，口齿清楚，有一定的语气。

Excellent: The test-taker is able to read using Putonghua. He or she does not drop characters, add characters, nor use the finger when reading; reads accurately, smoothly, with clear articulation and a degree of expression.

良: 能用普通话读。读的比较正确，流利，有的句子能读出语气，有个别差错。

Good: The test-taker is able to read using Putonghua. He or she reads relatively accurately, smoothly, and is able to read expressively some of the sentences but has a few mistakes.

中: 能读下来，但不流利，有多处错误，不能读出语气。

Average: The test-taker is able to read through the text, but not smoothly. He or she makes many mistakes and is unable to read expressively.

差: 读不成句，错误多。

Poor: The test-taker cannot complete sentences while reading and makes many mistakes.

Criteria for Speaking

优：　能看懂图意，用普通话完整，准确地说出三幅图的图意，口齿清楚。

Excellent:　The test-taker is able to understand the meaning of the pictures, to use Putonghua entirely, and to speak accurately about the content of the three pictures with clear articulation.

良：　能看懂图意，用普通话说出主要内容，但语句不够连贯。

Good:　The test-taker is able to understand the meaning of the pictures, and to use Putonghua to speak about the main points of the content, but the words and sentences lack coherence.

中：　能看懂图意，用普通话说出内容，但不够准确，清楚，语句不够通顺，连贯。

Average:　The test-taker is able to understand the meaning of the pictures, and to use Putonghua to speak about the content, but is not accurate and clear. His or her words and sentences lack fluency and coherence.

差：　看不懂图，说不清楚图上的内容，说不成句。

Poor:　The test-taker is unable to understand the meaning of the pictures, and cannot speak clearly about the pictures' content nor in complete sentences.

The kind of criteria presented above is not unfamiliar. It is roughly similar to criteria of other direct tests of oral proficiency around the world. However, there are details in the criteria that draw our attention.

In the Reading Aloud criteria for the Excellent level, there is a concern about dropping and adding characters. It is not clear what the test-makers intend here. The task of the reading aloud test is to read a passage in Hanyu Pinyin. There is little chance that the test-takers would be dropping or adding individual sounds. There is, however, a greater chance that test-takers may drop or add syllables. It would have been more precise if the test-makers had used the word *yīnjié* 音节 'syllable' or *cí* 词 'word.' Their choice of *zì* 字 implies a Chinese character perspective, in spite of the content of the test.

This perspective is seen again in the Reading Aloud test criteria where the Excellent and Good levels require reading in Putonghua. Since the reading is done with Hanyu Pinyin, it is hard to conceive how else other than in Putonghua that reading could be done. If the text were written in Chinese characters and the test-takers read the text in a variety other than Putonghua, then the criterion could be valid. But reading Chinese characters is not the content of the test. The only way for Putonghua not to be read is due to an inability to decode syllables written in Hanyu Pinyin because the system was not learned properly.

With the Speaking part, Putonghua is a relevant criterion. At the same time, it is a constant criterion for all but the Poor level. All levels have ranking criteria for delivery and coherence, but only the Poor level does not explicitly refer to Putonghua. This criterion is more stringent than for the assessment of elementary school teachers. Zhou Youguang (1986) provides criteria for three grades of Putonghua ability. Only the first grade requires a total use of Putonghua. The second and third grades allow for varying use of local speech varieties. For children, accuracy in Putonghua is stressed, as well as accuracy in writing Chinese characters.

Summary

The learning of Chinese characters constitutes the prototypical task of acquiring Chinese literacy. From here on, the pace of the class slowed down, for now the children were becoming truly literate. The children learned the names of the various strokes and how to write them in the correct order. To be able to remember them, especially to develop a productive knowledge of thousands of characters, a great deal of practice and rote learning are necessary.

Learning Chinese characters in the schools and with the official textbooks is not simply a matter of practicing calligraphy and learning characters in isolation. The curriculum groups the characters in meaningful sets, be they topical themes or semantic fields. Furthermore, the textbooks and tests require that Chinese character knowledge be contextual. Even during the first semester, children are expected to use Chinese characters in sentences.

The introduction of Chinese characters in the curriculum does not mean that speaking skills are undeveloped. Employing pictures provided in the textbook, pupils are continually encouraged to practice their Putonghua speaking skills. Just as the textbooks emphasize the functional use of Chinese characters, the illustrations in the textbooks, whether or not intended, depict realities of Chinese society, particularly in the realms of gender roles in the home, gender roles in careers, and socio-economic aspirations of an urban life style.

Chapter Six

Spheres of Literacy

In this chapter we analyze literacy, exploring its significance in the light of our findings. The *Collins Cobuild English language dictionary* (Sinclair, 1987, p. 849) simply defines literacy as "the ability to read and write." Despite this seemingly straightforward definition, the word has been used by governments, teachers, scholars, and activists in numerous contexts. *The literacy dictionary* (Harris & Hodges, 1995), for instance, provides at least 38 types of literacy. Like most forms of human behavior, the process of acquiring literacy and the context in which it is done are interrelated. The description of the interrelationship will provide the basis for our understanding of literacy. We attempt this by delineating literacy into three spheres of meaning.

The spheres of literacy can be analyzed in the following three ways. The first sphere is the task, referring to the requirements of language and script learning. The second sphere is the motivation, describing the reasons for acquiring literacy. The third sphere is the social and cultural identities that are assumed as a consequence of the acquisition of literacy.

The Task of Acquiring Literacy

In 1953, UNESCO drew up policies on literacy in The Monograph on Fundamental Education VIII: *The use of vernacular languages in education*. The document contains the following statement: "We take it as axiomatic that every child of school age should attend school and that every illiterate should be made literate. We take it as axiomatic, too, that the best medium for instruction is the mother

128

tongue of the child" (LePage, 1997, p. 4). In China today, most children may have access to school, but they do not necessarily have access to literacy through their mother tongue. The difference between mother tongue and standard language in China is a matter of degree, depending on geographical location and the nature of the local vernacular. To assist children in these situations, especially children who speak varieties of one of the Chinese dialect groups, we are not aware of official bilingual education programs to facilitate the literacy acquisition process. In contrast, we are aware that the government is not opposed to bilingual education among ethnic minorities. In some areas like Dehong County in southwestern Yunnan, bilingual education is promoted in only selected minority languages (Hong, 1998). In some areas where bilingual education has been provided, it is often the members of minority groups themselves who reject it out of fear it would hinder their children's academic achievement. This was the reaction among Zhuang nationality leaders in Guangxi Province (Lin, 1997). Hong Xiao (1998) concludes that the government, in taking a relatively moderate attitude toward the minority groups by allowing bilingual education to be offered, has become more successful in promoting Putonghua and Chinese-character writing instead of developing and maintaining minority literacy traditions.

Because many children in China do not speak standard Chinese at home, literacy acquisition in the schools involves not only learning to read and write, but also learning to speak the standard language. The task of learning to speak Putonghua in the schools is not carried out as an independent oral skills course. It is implemented together with the task of acquiring writing systems. The first system to learn is Hanyu Pinyin, a Roman script that phonemically represents Putonghua. Depending on the degree of difference between the local speech variety and Putonghua, first grade classes can spend a period ranging from 5 to 12 weeks to learn the Hanyu Pinyin system. This reality carries educational implications. There is roughly a seven-week difference between the time spent on Hanyu Pinyin and Putonghua instruction in Beijing and in parts of Guangdong Province. The dialect group areas are at a disadvantage with this extra time spent on language instruction. In spite of this reality, our students in Nanjing unanimously claimed that when they were school children, the Putonghua and Hanyu Pinyin learning process was never a problem for them. At the same time, one university colleague reported, that near Suzhou, subjects other than Chinese language were taught in the local Wu variety. Anna Kwan-Terry and K. K. Luke (1997) report that in remote areas, literacy is acquired in the local vernacular because of the unavailability of teachers who speak Putonghua. The extent to which education in the vernacular continues to exist in the dialect group areas of South China is a question that requires further study.

Once the Hanyu Pinyin system is learned, Chinese characters are taught with the assistance of Hanyu Pinyin. Although Chinese characters are presented in thematic groups, children do not know a sufficient number of them to read a continuous text. For that reason, there is an intertext stage where children read material written in both Hanyu Pinyin and Chinese characters. As more Chinese characters are learned, Hanyu Pinyin is used less and eventually its use for textual reading is discontinued. Its use, however, continues for various technical functions such as consulting reference material and word processing.

The task of learning more than one script cannot be evaluated only by the number of scripts. The nature of the scripts themselves has to be considered, especially as different kinds of scripts require different kinds of learning strategies. Alphabets possess the flexibility to adapt to different phonemic systems, yet spelling can be fossilized in pronunciation patterns of the past that have little phonemic relevance today. In addition, understanding the principles of an alphabet can often be too conceptual for children, although this did not pose a great difficulty among the classes we observed. The advantage of Hanyu Pinyin is that the phoneme-grapheme correspondences are highly regular. But as soon as the system is covered in class, the teacher moves on rapidly to present Chinese characters.

As a "morpheme-syllable writing system" (Coulmas, 1989, p. 107), Chinese characters possess initial advantages of learning. For instance, the syllable base of the characters allows for accurate modeling by the teacher. However, the sheer number of Chinese characters illustrates the burden of the task. Although some less difficult reading material is available in the bookstores, often with Hanyu Pinyin interspersed among Chinese characters, the task to achieve newspaper literacy will take at least another eight and a half years of schooling.

Motivations for Acquiring Literacy

Most children attending school have not decided to go on their own. Some children may look forward to the experience, but the decision to go rarely rests with them. In most cases, literacy is introduced to (or imposed on) children regardless of their initiative. The motivation, then, rests with the parents and society. Parents may have a variety of reasons. It could simply be based on doing what all the other children are doing and that not to participate might be seen as shameful. In a similar way, the motivation of parents could include the desire for social mobility. Academic achievement, the rewards of further education, and respected employment can enhance the family's prestige. The motivation could also be simply based on practical notions that it makes good sense to become literate because there are tangible returns ("Literacy Classes," 1994; Zhang Xia, 1994). The motivation, on the other hand, of society to offer school literacy is to provide a basic social service that is becoming widely viewed as a human right. But in China, school literacy has a more urgent dimension and that involves the motivation by society to use school literacy as a vehicle for national unity. Generally speaking, parents and society may agree that literacy acquired in standard forms is the kind of literacy that is worth having children learn.

We suggest, however, that even with a small degree of orthographic literacy, some benefits of literacy can be accessed. For children, as for anyone learning to read, the success of the acquisition process will be influenced by the speed with which the benefits are delivered. Part of the success of literacy in Japan is due to the amount of material available for beginning readers. However, access to interesting reading material is not the only motivating factor for acquiring literacy. There are functional motivations to achieve even partial literacy. The recognition of major place names can facilitate use of public transportation. The knowledge of names of businesses can help a person distinguish a restaurant from a barber shop. The ability to read telephone numbers for emergency services like the fire station or the police can be an asset. Various levels of functional literacy have existed in China, and although the extent and nature of the functionality is largely unknown, the fact that China has remained a political entity for over two millennia is partially due to the cohesive force of the Chinese language.

The existence of a range of literate abilities in the population is not new. There is evidence for varying literacy levels in early-modern Chinese society. Evelyn Rawski (1979) describes the situation by presenting four levels of literacy. The first level is the scholar, including both the successful and unsuccessful candidates in the civil service examinations. The second level includes merchants, artisans, and richer farmers who have a knowledge of several thousand characters and can perform many clerical functions. The third level includes those who received a minimal education in short-term programs like winter schools and have a knowledge of several hundred characters. The fourth level includes the illiterates. Rawski makes the point that in China, most people lived in proximity to literate persons, thus receiving many of the benefits that literacy provides.

The fact that most literate people in Qing dynasty China had varying degrees of literate ability means that they probably possessed adequate skills to perform certain functions. For economic reasons, it was the families that supported members to be educated. Chinese family units continue to play a powerful role in economic development today (Whyte, 1996). Economic motivation of families, however, does not always correlate with academic achievement. Some of the elementary school teachers complained that parents involved in small private businesses tended not to support their children's studies. In spite of these examples, pragmatic motivations continue to provide people with reasons for acquiring literacy.

A strong motivation that can encourage people to acquire literacy is ideology. Emancipatory literacy, for example, is based on the ideology that literacy must be available to all people, and that by becoming literate the people's social and economic livelihoods will improve. This kind of ideology motivated Chinese reformers like Qu Qiubai to develop an alphabet and disseminate it during the 1930s in the struggle for liberation from the oppressive social order. This kind of program is similar to the more recent efforts of Paolo Freire in Latin America. Another function of ideological literacy is to maintain and promote religious faith (Street, 1984). In fervent Muslim countries such as Iran, the primary function of literacy is to learn the Koran. In this context, to read the Koran provides not only knowledge of matters of faith, it also provides knowledge of appropriate civic behavior. For all religions that possess scriptures, there are examples where literacy is acquired for specific ideological aims.

The ideology of providing literacy in China includes the egalitarian notion that everyone should have the opportunity to learn the skill, but the ideology is less of an emancipatory one. Instead, the ideology is centered in consolidating and maintaining political unity and it is here where the state's reasons for providing literacy may not necessarily correspond with the individual's desire to become literate. However, motivation for acquiring literacy, especially in China, needs also to take into account reasons why access to literacy is provided. Ideological literacy is not new in China. The small class of highly literate scholars were well-versed in the Confucian texts which in turn constituted much of the content of the civil service examinations. Confucian ideology promoted submission to authority and a social structure based on specific kinds of relationships. Therefore, becoming familiar with these texts was seen as advantageous for maintaining the political and social status quo. Moreover, since these texts contained ethical content, readers were expected to think and act according to the intent of the texts. These kinds of expectations also exist in socities with literacies centered on the Bible or the Koran.

National unity in China is a genuine concern. There are the issues of unification with Taiwan and the integration of Hong Kong. The Tibet question and other ethnic tensions linger on the periphery. The economic disparity between the coastal areas and the interior results in great numbers of migrant workers who do not possess the right of abode in the areas in which they work. China is a vast country with a range of climates and terrain. It contains over a billion people in many ethnic groups that identify themselves to a greater or lesser degree as Chinese. A large number who identify themselves as Chinese speak mutually unintelligible language varieties.

Historically, China is the world's longest enduring empire. Except for brief disruptions consisting of a century or two or less, the Chinese empire has lasted for more than over 2000 years. Reformers since the late nineteenth century envisioned China as a modern nation. China as a nation, not an empire, is the model adopted by both the Republic of China and the People's Republic of China. For a modern nation, active participation or the impression of participation is an important attribute. Although both republics of China have been authoritarian for most of the twentieth century, each assumes a mandate of the people. To ensure the sense of participation, a national language is needed to provide not only communication on a national scale but also a sense of national identity.

We have explained in chapter one that the unity of the Chinese language was maintained in three ways through: (1) Chinese characters (2) Wenyan, literary Chinese and (3) Guanghua, the speech of the mandarins. These three are listed in order of cohesive strength. Of the three cohesive linguistic forces for national unity, Chinese characters have been historically the most powerful. They still are today. Since the 1911 Revolution, however, there has been a gradual effort to re-prioritize the cohesive forces, that is, to make the spoken language the primary force for unity, not the written language. It is for this reason that Putonghua is taught in schools, and reading and writing are taught in the context of the spoken standard language. This process emphasizes the proximity of the written language to the spoken, and that literacy is acquired through the vernacular. In other words, Putonghua is supposed to be the vernacular through which literacy is acquired. By becoming the means for acquiring Chinese characters, the most cohesive linguistic force for national unity, Putonghua's role in promoting national unity is strengthened.

Social and Cultural Identities in Acquiring Literacy

After the initial weeks of learning Putonghua and Hanyu Pinyin, the teachers announced to the pupils that they would now begin learning Chinese characters. This script is not like foreign scripts. This is China's own script. Moreover, to learn Chinese characters is to be identified as Chinese and true Chinese literacy is literacy in Chinese characters. It is not simply for national communication. The acquisition of literacy is participation in the cultural heritage: the learning of the strokes, the learning of stroke order, the learning of the radicals, the learning of brush calligraphy, and learning them all precisely. All these are segments of a process that constitute a tradition that is largely unbroken for over three millennia. To participate in this acquisition process is to participate in a literate tradition that reinforces the notion that knowledge of the script brings access to the entire literary tradition. Identifying with the nation's history and its culture presupposes a degree of knowledge about the literary tradition; consequently literacy is seen as prestigious.

The motivation to acquire literacy may not only be an attraction to the prestige, but a fear of shame for having not acquired it or having not acquired it properly. This, however, depends on the kind of literacy obtained. For instance, in Southern Hunan, a script known as the Women's Script developed over the centuries (Chiang, 1995). It was, as the name states, a script used only by women. Men could not read the script and preferred to use Chinese characters, which they considered more prestigious. Women's Script has all but died out as women have gained more access to schools and thus standard scripts. It is an accepted fact throughout the world that acquiring literacy can lead to academic achievement and thus more career options and social mobility. Usually this can only be achieved through standard forms of literacy.

Not all people are attracted by prestige. Daphne Key (1998) has described a phenomenon called "literacy shutdown." Certain people simply refuse to learn in response to the arrogance and power of people, like teachers, who insist on precise norms of literacy. Although her observations were in the North American context, we predict there may be similar kinds of reactions elsewhere in school literacy programs as well as nation-wide campaigns. It was not only among elementary school teachers in Nanjing that we observed attitudes towards precision. Newspapers frequently ran articles on prescriptive advice for proper linguistic expression (Zhu, 1991). At Zhejiang Normal University in Jinhua in the Wu dialect group area, for example, every classroom door had a label painted 讲普通话 写规范字 'speak Putonghua, write standard characters.' There were even billboards with this slogan around the campus to remind students. Another label we observed on the campus was 普通话是教师职业语言 'Putonghua is the professional language of teachers.' These kinds of reminders indicate that there are degrees of resistance to standard language forms both in speech and writing.

Who, then, speaks precise Putonghua? As they move up through elementary school, children's Putonghua skills gradually cease to be precise. As literacy increases, the focus of precision shifts from the dual emphasis on speech and writing to precision in writing. By lower middle school, teachers speak Putonghua with varying degrees of accuracy. When observing Chinese writing classes in an upper middle school in Nanjing to gather data on contrastive rhetoric, the "Chinese" teacher spoke Putonghua with such a strong local pronunciation, his lectures were almost entirely unintelligible to us. With the tendency of families, neighbors, as well as teachers to speak the local variety, it is natural that children, as they get older, lose their precision in Putonghua pronunciation.

Although Beijing is the center of government, its residents do not necessarily speak precise Putonghua. There are distinctive pronunciation features that characterize Beijing speech. Many Chinese people remark that residents of northeastern China speak Putonghua most accurately. Regardless of these informal observations, precise Putonghua is not marked by a specific region, except that certain regional varieties are seen to have a closer proximity. We can therefore say that the precise use of Putonghua remains the domain of media professionals, and elementary school teachers and pupils. Despite its official status, it follows that precise Putonghua is not seen as particularly prestigious. This illustrates a strong tendency toward solidarity. People tend to identify with their locality and thus with the local vernacular. If people speak Putonghua, it is done with local phonological characteristics. In Southern China, people often describe their Putonghua as *nánfāng pǔtōnghuà* 南方普通话 'southern Putonghua.' Despite the local characteristics in most speakers' Putonghua, the question remains as to the degree to which the speaker must code-switch. For speakers of the mutually unintelligible dialect groups of southern China, code-switching to Putonghua is like switching to a foreign language. In contrast, for residents of Beijing and parts of Northern China, code-switching is minimal.

This does not mean that prestige varieties do not exist in China. We have indicated that the Beijing variety has prestige because it is spoken in the capital. We have also pointed out that the regional dialects of Shanghai, Xiamen, and Guangzhou have prestige due to their economic status, together with, in the case of Xiamen and Guangzhou, their linguistic relationships to large communities in Taiwan and Hong Kong, as well as Singapore, Malaysia, and Indonesia. There may be other prestige varieties. Just from casual observation, we have noticed that the Putonghua pronunciation of many Nanjing residents tends to be similar to the pronunciation of Shanghai Putonghua speakers. This exists in spite of the fact that most Nanjing residents do not speak the Wu dialect. Could there be prestige varieties of Putonghua? Could a Nanjing resident, for example, who does not speak Wu, choose to speak Putonghua with Wu pronunciation patterns? More studies are needed to analyze these sociolinguistic patterns.

Some areas of China are trying to address the resistance to using standard language forms by offering instrumental motivation. The town of Huaxi in southern Jiangsu Province (also in the Wu dialect group area) has successfully taken advantage of the economic reforms and has become wealthy both in agriculture and industry. To encourage more people to speak Putonghua, they have offered a salary increase for those who can speak it well. The increase is doubled if a person can also speak a foreign language (Fu, 1992). Political reality also plays a role in motivating people to speak Putonghua. In Hong Kong, for example, Putonghua courses are compulsory for local government officials. Their language ability is further facilitated by government-sponsored trips into the provinces of China during which no translation services in Cantonese are provided ("HK Civil Servants," 1993). In addition to Putonghua, literacy skills are also used as an incentive. In response to increasing numbers of women from the provinces who are marrying Beijing men, city residents are supporting a plan to test these women's literacy skills before they receive their residency permits ("Efforts Made," 1991). These attempts suggest that identities other than a national identity exist and that these other identities present a challenge. To what degree these identities conflict with or complement each other is a matter for further research.

For children in the first-grade classroom in Nanjing, their social and cultural identities were not limited to the Chinese context. As they began learning Hanyu Pinyin, several children pointed out the similarity of Hanyu Pinyin letters to the letters of foreign languages. They also pointed out that the knowledge of these letters would help them learn foreign languages. They further suggested that a knowledge of foreign languages can lead to tangible benefits. In learning a Roman alphabet, the children perceived that they were assuming an identity in the global context.

Summary

Literacy has been described in terms of the following three spheres: the task, motivation, and social and cultural identity. In describing each one, the interrelationship of the three has become evident. For example, the task of acquiring literacy remains the way it is because: (a) the standard norms of writing carry the most prestige (b) the standard spoken language is used in the task to insure that speaking will be learned and (c) participating in the process of the task itself is an act of national identity.

The motivation to acquire literacy often differs from the motivation to provide opportunities for it. Individuals and families who wish to acquire literacy do so for practical reasons of social participation, but also for social mobility and increasing occupational options. Those who provide literacy, for example, governments and non-governmental organizations, do so for other reasons. These include citizen registration, national unity, health, and economic development. While economic development might be a cause shared by all parties, other motives shared by one or more parties may include individual and group empowerment, as well as faith and ideology.

As individuals become cognizant of the motivations for acquiring literacy, these motivations provide them with new identities and growth in existing identities. Participating in school literacy provides institutional identity. Literacy in a national language can lead to further awareness of national identity. Literacy for economic development can lead to occupational identities. With the skills of literacy, individuals possess the capacity to add to and alter their identities.

Chapter Seven

Conclusion

The central question that prompted our research was: How do young children in China acquire literacy skills in school? In short, children in China begin to learn to read in school using a Roman alphabet. The Hanyu Pinyin alphabet represents the phonemic system of Putonghua, standard Chinese. Having learned all possible syllables of Putonghua and some of its vocabulary, children then embark on a journey to master real Chinese literacy, that is literacy in Chinese characters. That the knowledge of Chinese characters is necessary for an individual to become literate in Chinese is a reality which goes back over 3000 years. What is different in the second half of the twentieth century is that the occasion for learning to read in the schools is used for the additional task of learning to speak the standard language. Children learn the pronunciation and vocabulary of the standard language, Putonghua, by learning the Hanyu Pinyin alphabet. This alphabet which is used to facilitate learning Putonghua and Chinese characters is largely discarded once the main script is learned, although the alphabet remains for certain functions. The Roman alphabet is revived, however, at the time the individual begins learning a foreign language, most commonly, English.

From our observations, the two schools were successful in carrying out their initial literacy education task. In six weeks, children had acquired literacy in Hanyu Pinyin. Both boys and girls achieved this goal. At Yizhongxin School, we were informed that all of the pupils except two, in a class of 55, scored over 80% on their tests. Our observations took place in schools with competent teachers. Despite the large classes, teachers employed a variety of techniques that attracted the children's attention. All the children had textbooks and exercise books. Most children had support for their studies from home. Although we have no direct data concerning home literacy, individual problems tended to be attributed, by teachers, to inadequate support from parents. Therefore, if competent teachers, materials, and support from home are available, the acquisition of literacy is possible in spite of the large class size.

Our study was conducted in an urban area of a relatively prosperous part of China. The problems of access to education, resulting in statistics of 25.8% illiteracy nationwide of which half are adult women (Greaney, 1996), seemed far removed from Nanjing. The urban environment in which these two schools existed was similar to the kind of urban environments that dominate textbook illustrations. From that standpoint, the reality we observed may be close to the ideal social environment most Chinese people aspire to. Moreover, the initial success of the two schools could also be attributed to the positive working environments that their administrations have endeavored to create. Specifically, both schools had access to extra funds; therefore issues of teacher compensation and facility maintenance were handled expeditiously. The teachers responded with a positive attitude toward their work.

At the same time, we did not observe the entire literacy acquisition process. We only observed the teaching of Putonghua, Hanyu Pinyin, and the beginning of Chinese character instruction. What happens beyond this stage, and whether or not serious problems exist, we do not know. How children perform after having learned Chinese characters in schools is a matter for further research. Conducting research in China, particularly qualitative research, is not an easy task. There are difficulties gaining access to both people and institutions. Furthermore, the information gathered from one source is often in conflict with information gathered from other sources. It is even difficult to obtain reliable statistics, thus posing perils for most researchers (see Henze, 1987; Price, 1981; Rosen, 1987).

In our introduction, we described a Ms. Chen, who, with limited literacy skills, was able to establish and run a successful painting business. We emphasized the point that she represented a view in Chinese society that literacy skills are not necessary to be successful economically. For that reason, millions of people across China, especially girls, are dropping out of school to engage in income-generating work. One estimate indicates that 400 million children aged 18 and under constitute one-third of the total population. The annual school dropout rate is four million, of which 83% are girls (Xie, 1991). As a result, it is claimed that on the average, a Chinese person receives 5 years of schooling compared with 12 years, on the average, for a Japanese person (R. Wang, 1990). Moreover, over 25% of the world's illiterates live in China (Carceles, 1990).

What we did not emphasize about Ms. Chen is her partial literacy. She was not illiterate. The fact that she lacked basic productive literacy skills does not mean she lacked in receptive skills: She knew what her name looked like. And what more did she know? The existence of people with partial literacy skills is not new. Perhaps these people have contributed to the tenacity of a script or a writing style just as much as those who learned the script and had access to the quantity of literature written in it.

Quantity of literature and history are attributes, in addition to pervasive use, that offer the writing system and textual style prestige and thus attract people to learn it. One of the reasons for acquiring literacy in a particular script is the access it provides to the literature of a cultural tradition. A strong motivation for maintaining Chinese characters in China and in Japan is because of the access the literacy skill provides to the long tradition. Insup Taylor, for example, claims that a knowledge of Chinese characters provides her with access to the works of Confucius (Taylor & Taylor, 1995). She shares a perception of many who are literate in Chinese characters that they have access to all texts written in the script. The chances are they may need help to comprehend many texts, just as those literate in English may not understand English texts in all fields and through history. At the same time, they feel they have the potential to be literate, given a little time and effort. Many well-educated people who use personal computers, for example, would rather not struggle through a computer manual to solve a problem or learn how to do something new. Rather, they tend to ask for help and receive oral instructions from a more expert person. Few would admit they are incapable of reading a manual, but they would prefer not to exert the effort. We are not questioning whether the person is able or willing to read. Rather, we are questioning what being literate implies. The confidence that comes from the

142

perception that an entire literary tradition is accessible is perhaps the unstated goal of literacy education. This confidence provides a sense of satisfaction for those who are already literate. This confidence becomes an object of prestige for those who wish to acquire literacy.

We have described in detail the task of acquiring literacy in Chinese schools. Although there may be regional variations in the details of how this task is achieved, Chinese children, making up the largest single language group in the world, acquire literacy in this manner. The Hanyu Pinyin script was acquired with a great deal of success in a short time. However, this is only the initial stage of literacy.

The problem with the script is that it lacks practical use. If a person wishes to communicate throughout China, Putonghua is sufficient for oral communication, even spoken with local characteristics. If one needs to write, Chinese characters are a better vehicle of communication for they transcend different speech varieties, intelligible or otherwise. If Hanyu Pinyin is used, at least today, one needs to remember precise Putonghua to write it and the reader must remember precise Putonghua to comprehend it. These conditions, however, are the same for any writing system with alphabetic spelling. The difference is that most people have not maintained their knowledge of how Putonghua is spelled. This reality is acutely felt by people experiencing difficulty in word processing using Hanyu Pinyin to enter Chinese character text.

Another reason why Hanyu Pinyin spelling is often not retained is that the writing system lacks sufficient prestige. For many people, it is soon replaced by the English alphabet as a script for communication. The amount of literature available in Hanyu Pinyin is small. Therefore, one cannot access the literary tradition through it. In spite of their difficult nature and the time consumed in learning them, Chinese characters remain the core of Chinese literacy today. The fact that they do, despite the many arguments for reform, reflects a basic principle about literacy. People will tend to choose the prestige script when making the investment in literacy.

In Imperial China, the unity of the nation was promoted by the written language. Today, unity is promoted by both the written and spoken language. Given the multilingual situation of China, promoting unity through both modes is an enormous task. To ensure that the task is carried out, the occasion for learning to read in schools is maximized to include learning the standard spoken language. In this way, the age-old prestige of Chinese characters is shared with Putonghua, so that the motivation to acquire the writing system can also be shared with learning the standard spoken language.

Appendix

Table A1

Comparison of Hanyu Pinyin Initials with IPA, Wade-Giles, and English

Hanyu Pinyin	IPA	Wade-Giles	English
b	p	p	spot
p	p′	p′	paper
m	m	m	melon
f	f	f	favor
d	t	t	start
t	t′	t′	take
n	n	n	name
l	l	l	lake
z	ts	ts	pleasant
zi	tsɿ	tsŭ	zoo
c	ts′	ts′	Betsy
ci	tsɿ′	tz′ŭ	bets-a-lot
s	s	s	song
si	sɿ	ssŭ, szŭ	sit
zh	tʂ	ch	general
zhi	tʂl	chih	German
ch	tʂ l	ch′	challenge
chi	ʂ	ch′ih	chirp
sh	ʂ l	sh	ship
shi	ʐ	shih	sure
r	ʐ l	j	rouge
ri	tɕ	jih	earth
j	tɕi	ch	jail
ji	tɕy	chi	gee
ju	tɕ′	chü	judicial
q	tɕ′i	ch′	cherub
qi	tɕ′y	ch′i	cheese
qu	ɕ′	ch′ü	choose
x	ɕi	hs	shout
xi	ɕy	hsi	she
xu	k	hsü	shoot
g	k′	k	skip
k	x	k′	cake
h	j	h	hair
y	w	y	yet
w		w	wet

Table A2

Comparison of Hanyu Pinyin Finals with IPA, Wade-Giles, and English

Hanyu Pinyin	IPA	Wade-Giles	English
a	a	a	alarm
o	o	o	oak
e	ɤ	ê	bull
er	ər	êrh	car
ai	ai	ai	buy
ei	ei	ei	bay
ao	au	ao	bough
ou	ou	ou	bow
an	an	an	ban
en	ən	ên	redden
ang	ɑŋ	ang	song
eng	əŋ	êng	sung
ong	uŋ	ung	Bayonne
i	i	i	he
ia	ia	ia	Ethiopia
ie	iɛ	ieh	near
iao	iau	iao	yowl
iu	iou	iu	row
ian	iɛn	ien	yen
in	in	in	Jean
iang	iɑŋ	iang	neon
ing	iŋ	ing	raging
iong	iuŋ	iung	young
u	u	u	do
ua	ua	ua	Du Bois
uo	uo	uo	buoyant
uai	uai	uai	twilight
ui	ui	ui	tweed
uan	uan	uan	swan
un	un	un	tune
uang	uaŋ	uang	wrong
ü (yu)	y	(yün)	
üe (yue)	yɛ	üeh (y_)	(no umlauts in
üan (yuan)	yɛn	üan (yüan)	English)
ün (yun)	yn	ün (yün)	

Glossary

Alphabet, a script with symbols representing individual sounds of a particular language.

Baihua, (báihuà) 白话 literature based on the vernacular. It also refers to a literary genre of works written by authors active in the May Fourth Movement.

Bilabial sounds, are made with both lips (e.g., [p] and [b]).

Cadre, an official related to the Communist Party who assists in the administration of every danwei.

Ci, (cí) 词 word.

Content words, words in a language which carry the intended meaning, that is, the content, in contrast with function words which carry grammatical meaning.

Danwei, (dānwèi) 单位 a self-contained work unit (e.g., factory, office, or institution) offering housing, health, and education to all who are related with it.

Diglossia, a situation where speakers use both a prestige variety of a language as well as one or more other varieties.

Diphthong, two vowels together in a sequence of sounds (e.g., sane [ei]).

Difanghua, (dìfānghuà) 地方话 local speech.

Fangyan, (fāngyán) 方言 dialect.

Fantizi, (fántǐzì) 繁体字 the older (more complex) standard forms of Chinese characters, still used in Taiwan and Hong Kong.

Function words, words in a language that serve grammatical functions.

Gaige Kaifang, (gǎigé kāifāng) 改革开放 the policy of Reform and Opening to the Outside World begun in 1978 that is attributed to Deng Xiaoping.

Getihu, (gètǐhù) 个体户 small private business.

Grapheme, is the symbolic representation of a phoneme. In a spelling system like English, there can be multiple graphemes for a single phoneme. In a more efficient system like Hanyu Pinyin, there is almost a one-to-one correspondence of phonemes and graphemes.

Guanhua, (guānhuà) 官話 the mandarin Chinese of Imperial China.

Guanxi, (guānxì) 关系 social connections.

Guoyeu Romatzyh, (guóyǔ luómǎzì) 國語羅馬字 an official romanization developed in the 1920s that represented tones directly in the spelling.

Guoyin Zimu, (guóyīn zìmǔ, kuoyin tzumu) 國音字母 an alphabet for Chinese employing symbols derived from Chinese characters.

Guoyu, (guóyǔ, kuoyü) 國語 national language, pronounced as *kokugo* in Japanese.

Hanyu Pinyin, (hànyǔ pīnyīn) 汉语拼音 the Roman alphabet that phonemically represents Putonghua. Tones are represented by diacritic symbols over vowels.

Hiragana, one syllabary of Japanese that represents function words and content words with Japanese roots and older continental loan words.

Hanzi, (hànzì) 汉字 Chinese characters.

Homonyms, are different words that have the same sound, also called homophones.

Iconic, refers to the concreteness of a symbol. Most characters in writing systems are symbolic, thus abstract. Some pictographic characters and onomatopoeic expressions maintain degrees of iconicity, that is, possessing in the linguistic representation physical elements of their meaning.

Ideographic characters, one character represents one idea.

International Phonetic Alphabet (IPA), an alphabetic system designed to transcribe objectively any linguistic sound.

Jiantizi, (jiǎntǐzì) 简体字 standard simplified Chinese characters used in the People's Republic of China.

Kana, the two syllabaries of Japanese, Hiragana and Katakana.

Katakana, one syllabary of Japanese that is used for words of emphasis and foreign loan words including recent continental borrowings.

Ladinghua Xin Wenzi, (lādīnghuà xin wénzì, Latinxua Sin Wenz) 拉丁化新文字 the Roman alphabet developed in the 1920s by Qu Qiubai and others to promote literacy among Chinese immigrants in Russia.

Logographic characters, one character represents one word.

Meiji, the reign of Japan's reformist Emperor Meiji (1868-1912).

Metalanguage, the discourse of describing language (language about language).

Min, (mǐn) 闽 the group of dialects spoken in the region of Fujian Province and Taiwan.

Mnemonic devices, are strategies for memorizing information.

Monothong, a single vowel in a sequence of sounds (e.g., b<u>a</u>t [æ]).

Morpheme, is a unit of meaning. For example, the word "skipped" has two morphemes: *skip* and *-ed*. Some morphemes are free forms, capable of standing alone as words. Others are bound forms and must be linked to other morphemes. The study of the configurations of morphemes in a language is called morphology.

Moxie, (mòxiě) 默写 writing from memory or dictation.

Phoneme or **phonemic,** refers to the significant sounds of a particular language. An efficient alphabet represents only the phonemes of a language. In contrast, the International Phonetic Alphabet attempts to represent all existing linguistic sounds. No single language ever uses the whole set of sounds.

Phonics, a method of teaching reading that emphasizes the relationship between the sound and symbol in the alphabet. Words are then learned by pronouncing the letters that make up the words.

Pictographic characters, contain elements of the physical shape of the meaning they represent.

Protoliteracy, the original forms of writing in a language, for example, the ancient pictographic scripts that led to the development of Chinese characters.

Putonghua, (pūtōnghuà) 普通话 Mandarin Chinese, the standard language of the People's Republic of China.

Qing, 清 the final dynasty of Imperial China (1644-1911).

Radical, the classifying portion of a Chinese character.

Roman letters or **romanization,** alphabetic scripts based on Roman writing.

Syllabary, a script with symbols representing whole syllables.

Tianzige, (tiánzìgé) 填字格 ruled squares to practice writing Chinese characters with consistent proportions.

Velar sounds, are made with the back of the tongue near or touching the soft palate (e.g., [h], [k], and [g] are velar sounds).

Wade-Giles, the name of a romanized alphabet that was developed by Thomas F. Wade in 1867 and revised by Herbert A. Giles in 1912 (Taylor & Taylor, 1995, p. 124). Internationally, it has been the most widely used romanization system of Chinese, although recently Hanyu Pinyin has become the dominant system.

Wenyan, (wényán) 文言 classical written Chinese text.

Whole-word, a method of teaching reading using the recognition of words, not by the analysis of composite sounds as in phonics.

Wu, (wú) 吴 the group of dialects spoken in the Yangzi river delta region, including the dialect spoken in the city of Shanghai.

Yinjie, (yīnjié) 音节 syllable.

Yuwen, (yǔwén) 语文 school subject for Chinese language.

Zhihu, (zhíhū) 直呼 a method of teaching reading through phonics.

Zhuyin Fuhao, (zhùyīn fúhào, chuyin fuhao) 注音符號 another name for Guoyin Zimu. It is still used in Taiwan, popularly called "bopomofo."

Zi, (zǐ) 字 a letter or character in any script, but prototypically, a Chinese character.

Bibliography

Alitto, S. B. (1969). The language issue in Communist Chinese education. *Comparative Education Review, 13*, 43-59.

Allen, J. R. (1984). Chinese script and lexicography for the uninitiated. *Journal of the Chinese Language Teachers Association, 19*(3), 35-66.

Allen, K. (1998). Literacy and schooling in the United States of America *Visio, 25*, 85-94.

Allen, K. & Ingulsrud, J. E. (1998). What do you want to be when you grow up? An analysis of primary school textbooks in the People's Republic of China. *Journal of Multicultural, Multilingual Development, 20*(3), 171-181.

Allen, K. & Ingulsrud, J. E. (1996). Alphabetic biliteracy among children in China: The interface of English and Hanyu Pinyin. In M. Khoo, J. I. Lee, & A. Lim (Eds.), *Literacy and Biliteracy in Asia: Problems and issues in the next decade: Asian Reading Congress 1995 Selected Papers* (pp. 63-80). Singapore: National Book Development Council of Singapore.

Allington, R. L. & Walmsley, S. A. (Eds.). (1995). *No quick fix: Rethinking literacy programs in America's elementary schools*. New York: Teachers College Press.

Altbach, P. G., Arnove, R. F., & Kelly, G. P. (Eds.). (1982). *Comparative Education*. New York: Macmillan.

Arnove, R. F. (1984). A comparison of the Chinese and Indian education systems. *Comparative Education Review, 28*(3), 379-401.

Bao, Z. (1988). The syllable in Chinese. *Journal of Chinese Linguistics, 24*(2), 312-353.

Barton, D. (1994). *Literacy: An introduction to the ecology of the written language*. Oxford: Blackwell.

Bartsch, R. (1987). *Norms of language*. New York: Longman.

Bauer, J., Wang, F., Riley, N. E., & Zhao, X. (1992). Gender inequality in urban China. *Modern China, 18*(3), 333-370.

Bennett, G. (Ed.). (1996). *China facts and figures annual handbook, 20*. Gulf Breeze, FL: Academic International Press.

Blueprint for 20m to learn the three Rs. (1992, February 7). *China Daily*.

Bo, W. (1991, June 20). School's out but tutors at home are all the rage. *China Daily*, p. 6.

Bond, H. (Ed.). (1986). *The psychology of the Chinese people*. New York: Oxford University Press.

Brown, H. O. (1986). Primary schooling and the rural responsibility system in the People's Republic of China. *Comparative Education Review, 30*(3), 373-387.

Brown, J., Goodman, K. S., & Marek, A. M. (1996). *Studies in miscue analysis: An annotated bibliography*. Newark, DE: International Reading Association.

Brown, R. & Gilman, A. (1960). The pronouns of power and solidarity. In T. A. Sebeok (Ed.), *Style in language* (pp. 253-276). Cambridge, MA: MIT Press.

Burgess, C. S. (1975). *Decision-making in the educational system in selected cities of the People's Republic of China*. Unpublished doctoral dissertation, Fordham

152

University, New York.

Campaign to guard education. (1992, June 30). *China Daily.*

Campbell, R. (Ed.). (1998). *Facilitating preschool literacy.* Newark, DE: International Reading Association.

Carceles, G. (1990). World literacy prospects at the turn of the century: Is the objective of literacy for all by the year 2000 statistically plausible? *Comparative Education Review, 34*(1), 4-20.

Chan, M. K. M. & He, B. (1988). A study of the one thousand most frequently used Chinese characters and their simplification. *Journal of the Chinese Language Teachers Association, 23*(3), 49-68.

Chao, Y. R. (1968). Interlingual and interdialectal borrowings in Chinese. *Unicorn, 2,* 1-19.

Chen, E. S. H. (1988). Functional theoretical perspectives on the "modernization" of the Chinese language. *Journal of Chinese Linguistics, 16* (1), 125-150.

Chen, H. C. & Tzeng, O. (Eds.). (1992). *Language processing in Chinese.* Amsterdam, NL: Elsevier.

Chen, M. J., Yung, Y. F., & Ng, T. W. (1988). The effect of context on perception of Chinese characters. In I. M. Liu, H. C. Chen, & M. J. Chen (Eds.), *Cognitive aspects of the Chinese language, 1* (pp. 27-39). Hong Kong: Asian Research Service.

Chen, S. (1996). Reinvigorating ethnic cultural identity through mother-tongue teaching materials in Taiwan. *Language, Culture and Curriculum, 9*(3), 254-259.

Chen, S. H. (1973). Language and literature under Communism. In Yuanli Wu (Ed.), *China: A handbook* (pp. 705-715). New York: Praeger.

Cheng, C. (1985). *Contradictions in Chinese language reform* (Tech. Rep. No. LLL-T-7-85). Urbana: University of Illinois.

Cheng, C. & Shih, S. (1988). The nature of lexical access in Chinese: Evidence from experiments on visual and phonological priming in lexical judgement. In I. M. Liu, H. C. Chen, & M. J. Chen (Eds.), *Cognitive aspects of the Chinese language, 1* (pp. 1-14). Hong Kong: Asian Research Service.

Cheng, K. M. (1986). China's recent education reform: The beginning of an overhaul. *Comparative Education, 22*(3), 255-269.

Cheng, K. M. (1994). Young adults in a changing socialist society: Post-compulsory education in China. *Comparative Education, 30*(1), 63-73.

Chiang, W. W. (1995). *"We two know the script; we have become good friends," Linguistic and social aspects of the women's script literacy in southern Hunan, China.* New York: University Press of America.

China facts & figures annual (18). (1994). Gulf Breeze, FL: Academic International Press.

China starts education program. (1996, June 9). *The Daily Yomiuri.*

Chow, R. (1991). *Woman and Chinese modernity: The politics of reading between east and west.* Minneapolis: University of Minnesota Press.

Clemeston, J. (1996, October 21). Babbling masses. *Newsweek, 128*(17), p. 25.

Cleverly, J. (1984). Ideology and practice: A decade of change and continuity in contemporary Chinese education. *Comparative Education, 20*(1), 107-116.

A concise Chinese-English dictionary. (1991). Beijing: The Commercial Press.

Coulmas, F. (1989). *The writing systems of the world.* Oxford: Basil Blackwell.

Croll, E. (1995). *Changing identities of Chinese women.* Hong Kong: Hong Kong University Press.

Dai, B. Y. & Lu, J. P. (1985). Reading reform in Chinese primary schools.

153

Prospects, 15(1), 103-110.
DeFrancis, J. (1984). *The Chinese language: Fact and fantasy.* Honolulu: University of Hawaii Press.
DeFrancis, J. (1986). Graphic representation of Chinese tones. *Journal of the Chinese Language Teachers Association, 21*(2), 27-42.
DeFrancis, J. (1989). *Visible speech: The diverse oneness of writing systems.* Honolulu: University of Hawaii Press.
DeFrancis, J. (1996). Chinese lexicography at the crossroads. *Journal of the Chinese Language Teachers Association, 31*(3), 1-9.
Delany, B. & Paine, L. W. (1991). Shifting patterns of authority in Chinese schools. *Comparative Education Review, 35*(1), 23-43.
Deng tells TV announcers to slow down. (1993, February 5). *The Standard,* p. 5.
Dimmok, C. A. J., O'Donoghue, T. A., & Robb, A. S. (1996). Parental involvement in schooling: An emerging research agenda. *Compare, 26* (1), 5-20.
Downing, J. (1973). *Comparative reading: Cross-national studies of behavior and processes in reading and writing.* New York: Macmillan.
Durkin, D. (1993). *Teaching them to read* (6th ed.). Boston: Allyn & Bacon.
Education essentials. (1993, March 6). *China Daily,* p. 4.
Education reforms lie in diversifying system. (1994, March 31). *China Daily,* p. 4.
Efforts made to wipe out illiteracy. (1991, April 23). *China Daily.*
Everson, M. E. (1988). Speed and comprehension in reading Chinese: Romanization vs. characters revisited. *Journal of the Chinese Language Teachers Association, 23*(2), 1-15.
Fairbank, J. K. (1992). *China: A new history.* Cambridge, MA: Harvard University Press.
Fang, S. P., Horng, R. Y., & Tzeng, O. (1986). Consistency effects in the Chinese character pseudo-character naming tasks. In H. S. R. Kao & R. Hoosain (Eds.), *Linguistics, psychology, and the Chinese language* (pp. 11-21). Hong Kong: University of Hong Kong.
Fasold, R. (1984). *The sociolinguistics of society.* New York: Basil Blackwell.
Ferguson, C. A. (1959). Diglossia. *Word, 15,* 325-340.
Fishman, J. A. (1966). *Language loyalty in the United States.* The Hague: Mouton.
Flores d'Arcais, G. B. (1992). Graphemic, phonological, and semantic activation processes during the recognition of Chinese characters. In H. C. Chen & O. Tzeng (Eds.), *Language processing in Chinese* (pp. 37-66). Amsterdam, NL: Elsevier.
Fu, Z. Putonghua. (1992, May 18). *China Daily.*
Gardner, H. (1989). *To open minds.* New York: HarperCollins.
Gerbault, J. (1997). Pedegogical aspects of vernacular literacy. In A.Tabouret-Keller, R. B. Le Page, P. Gardener-Chloros, & G. Varro (Eds.), *Vernacular literacy* (pp. 142-186). New York: Oxford University Press.
Gfeller, E. (1997). Why should I learn to read? Motivations for literacy acquisition in a rural education programme. *International Journal of Educational Development, 17* (1), 101-112.
Gilmartin, C. K., Hershatter, G., Rofel, L., & White, T. (Eds.). (1994). *Engendering China: Women, culture, and the state.* Cambridge, MA: Harvard University Press.
Gong, Q. Deputies urge more input to education. (1993, March 27). *China Daily.*
Gong, Q. Accent put on standard Mandarin. (1994, June 26). *China Daily.*

154

Goodman, K. (1992). Whole language research: Foundations and development. In S. J. Samuels & A. E. Farstrup (Eds.), *What research has to say about reading instruction* (2nd ed., pp. 46-69). Newark, DE: International Reading Association.

Gottlieb, N. (1995). *Kanji politics: Language policy and Japanese script*. London: Kegan Paul.

Graves, M. F., Van Den Broek, P., & Taylor, B. M. (Eds.). (1996). *The first R: Every child's right to read*. New York: Teachers College Press.

Graves, M. F. & Dykstra, R. (1997). Contextualizing the first-grade studies: What is the best way to teach children to read? *Reading Research Quarterly, 32*(4), 342-344.

Greaney, V. (Ed.). (1996). *Promoting reading in developing countries*. Newark, DE: International Reading Association.

Hall, K. (1998). Critical literacy and the case for it in the early years of school. *Language, Culture and Curriculum, 11*(2), 183-194.

Hannas, W. C. (1997). *Asia's orthographical dilemma*. Honolulu: University of Hawaii Press.

Hanyu fangyan gaiyao 汉语方言概要 [survey of Chinese dialects] (1989). Beijing: Wenzi Gaige Chubanshe.

Hanyu fangyan zihui 汉语方言字汇 [lexicon of Chinese dialects] (1989). Beijing: Wenzi Gaige Chubanshe.

Harris, T. L. & Hodges, R. E. (1995). *The literacy dictionary: The vocabulary of reading and writing*. Newark, DE: International Reading Association.

Haugen, E. (1966). Language, dialect, nation. *American Anthropologist, 68*(4), 922-935.

Hawkins, J. N. (1978). National-minority education in the People's Republic of China. *Comparative Education Review, 22*(1), 147-162.

Hawkins, J. N. (1988). The transformation of education for rural development in China. *Comparative Education Review, 32*(3), 266-280.

Hawkins, J. N. & Stites, R. (1991). Strengthening the future's foundation: Elementary education reform in the People's Republic of China. *The Elementary School Journal, 92*(1), 41-60.

Hayes, E. B. (1987). The relationship between Chinese character complexity and character recognition. *Journal of the Chinese Language Teachers Association, 22*(2), 45-57.

Hayhoe, R. (1986). Penetration or mutuality? China's educational cooperation with Europe, Japan, and North America. *Comparative Education Review, 30*(4), 532-559.

He, J. Old characters pose a problem. (1993, April 12). *China Daily*.

Heath, S. B. (1983). *Ways with words*. Cambridge: Cambridge University Press.

Henze, J. (1987). Statistical documentation in Chinese education: Where reality ends and the myths begin. *Canadian and International Education, 16*(1), 198-210.

Hill, C. & Parry, K. (1994). Models of literacy: The nature of reading tests. In C. Hill & K. Parry (Eds.), *From testing to assessment* (pp. 7-34). New York: Longman.

HK civil servants learning *putonghua*. (1993, May 21). *China Daily*.

Ho, C. S. & Bryant, P. (1997). Learning to read beyond the logographic phase. *Reading Research Quarterly, 32*(3), 276-289.

Ho, S. H. (1976). Comments on teaching Chinese reading. *Journal of the Chinese Language Teachers Association, 11*(1), 52-57.

155

Homework to be cut for primary students. (1992, March 10). *China Daily*.
Hong, X. (1998). Minority languages in Dehong, China: Policy and reality. *Journal of Multilingual and Multicultural Development, 19*(3), 221-235.
Honig, E. (1992). *Creating Chinese ethnicity: Subei people in Shanghai 1850-1980*. New Haven, CT: Yale University Press.
Honig, E. & Hershatter, G. (1988). *Personal voices: Chinese women of the 1980's*. Stanford, CA: Stanford University Press.
Hoosain, R. (1992). Psychological reality of the word in Chinese. In H. C. Chen & O. Tzeng (Eds.), *Language processing in Chinese* (pp. 111-130). Amsterdam, NL: Elsevier.
Hoover-Dempsey, K. V. & Sandler, H. M. (1995). Parental involvement in children's education: Why does it make a difference? *Teachers College Record, 97*(2), 308-331.
Hsu, V. (1979). The current state of language reform and the teaching of language in the PRC. *Journal of the Chinese Language Teachers Association, 19*(3), 61-89.
Hu, C. T. (1984). The historical background: Examinations and control in pre-modern China. *Comparative Education, 20*(1), 7-25.
Hu, S. M. & Seifman, E. (Eds.). (1976). *Toward a new world outlook: A documentary history of education in the People's Republic of China, 1949-1976*. New York: AMS Press.
Hu, Y. (Ed.). (1962). *Xiandai hanyu* 现代汉语 [modern Chinese] Shanghai: Shanghai Jiaoyu Chubanshe.
Huang, J. (1987). *Hanyu fangyanxue* 汉语方言学 [Chinese dialectology]. Xiamen: Xiamen Daxue Chuban.
Huang, J. T. & Liu, I. M. (1978). Paired-associate learning proficiency as a function of frequency count, meaningfulness, and imagery value in Chinese two-character ideograms. *Acta Psychologica Taiwanica, 20*, 5-17.
Huang, J. T. & Wang, M. Y. (1992). From unit to gestalt: Perceptual dynamics in recognizing Chinese characters. In H. C. Chen & O. Tzeng (Eds.), *Language processing in Chinese* (pp. 3-36). Amsterdam, NL: Elsevier.
Huang, Z. Excessive homework is stifling our kids. (1994, June 22). *China Daily*.
Hunter, J. (1984). *The gospel of gentility: American women missionaries in turn-of-the-century China*. New Haven, CT: Yale University Press.
Indrisano, R. & Chall, J. S. (1995). Literacy development. *Journal of Education, 177*(1), 63-83.
Ingulsrud, J. E. (1994). Entrance test to Japanese universities: Social and historical context. In C. Hill & K. Parry (Eds.), *From testing to assessment* (pp. 61-81). New York: Longman.
Ingulsrud, J. E. (1996). Inservice teacher education: Engaging the dialogic communities of teachers. *Language, Culture, and Curriculum, 9*(2), 176-186.
Iwata, M. (1984). Kanji versus Kana: Neuropsychological correlates of the Japanese writing system. *Trends in Neurosciences, 7*, 290-293.
Jianming hanying cidian 简明汉英词典 [a concise Chinese-English dictionary]. (1991). Beijing: Commercial Press
Johnson, L.C. (Ed.). (1993). *Cities of Jiangnan in late imperial China*. Albany, NY: SUNY Press.
Kao, H.S.R. & Hoosain, R. (Eds.). (1986). *Linguistics, psychology, and the Chinese language*. Hong Kong: University of Hong Kong.
Karlgren, B. (1991). *Analytic dictionary of Chinese and Sino-Japanese*.

156

Minneola, NY: Dover. (Original work published 1923)

Karlgren, B. (1929). *Sound and symbol in Chinese.* London: Oxford University Press.

Key, D. (1998). *Literacy shutdown: Stories of six American women.* Newark, DE: International Reading Association.

Kids scold cadres for using cars. (1993, October 25). *China Daily.*

King, E. (1984). Chinese educational development in comparative perspective. *Comparative Education, 20*(1), 165-181.

King, P. L. (1983). Contextual factors in Chinese Pinyin writing. (Doctoral dissertation, Cornell University, 1983). *University Microfilms International* No. 8321888.

Kipnis, A. B. (1996). The language of gifts: Managing *guanxi* in a north China village. *Modern China, 22*(3), 285-314.

Kohut, J. Keeping the symbols simple in Beijing's war of words. (1991, April 6). *South China Morning Post.*

Kwan-Terry, A. & Luke, K. K. (1997). Tradition, trial, and error: Standard and vernacular literacy in China, Hong Kong, Singapore, and Malaysia. In A. Tabouret-Keller, R. B. Le Page, P. Gardener-Chloros, & G. Varro (Eds.), *Vernacular literacy* (pp. 271-315). New York: Oxford University Press.

Kwo, O. W. Y. (1989). Language education in a changing economic and political context: The teaching of Putonghua in Hong Kong schools. *Journal of Multilingual and Multicultural Development, 10*(4), 297-306.

Kwong, J. (1979). The educational experiment of the Great Leap Forward, 1958-1959: Its inherent contradictions. *Comparative Education Review, 23*(3), 443-455.

Kwong, J. (1985). Changing political culture and changing curriculum: An analysis of language textbooks in the People's Republic of China. *Comparative Education, 21*(2), 197-208.

Kwong, J. & Xiao, H. (1989). Educational equality among China's minorities. *Comparative Education, 25*(2), 229-243.

Labov, W. (1972). *Sociolinguistic patterns.* Philadelphia: University of Pennsylvania Press.

LePage, R. B. (1964). *The national language question.* London: Oxford University Press.

LePage, R. B. (1997). Introduction. In A. Tabouret-Keller, R. B. Le Page, P. Gardener-Chloros, & G. Varro (Eds.), *Vernacular literacy* (pp. 1-20). New York: Oxford University Press.

LePage, R. B. & Tabouret-Keller, A. (1985). *Acts of identity.* Cambridge: Cambridge University Press.

Leseman, P. & de Jong, P. F. (1998). Home Literacy: Opportunity, instruction, cooperation, and social-emotional quality predicting early reading achievement. *Reading Research Quarterly, 33*(3), 294-319.

Levine, D. R. & Adelman, M. B. (1993). *Beyond language: Cross-cultural communication* (2nd ed.). Englewood Cliffs, NJ: Prentice Hall.

Levine, K. (1986). *The social context of literacy.* New York: Routledge & Kegan Paul.

Lewin, K. & Xu, H. (1989). Rethinking revolution: Reflections on China's 1985 educational reforms. *Comparative Education, 25*(1), 7-17.

Lewin, K. M., Xu, H., Little, A., & Zheng, J. (1994). *Educational innovation in China: Tracing the impact of the 1985 reforms.* Harlow, UK: Longman.

Li, J. & Har, J. (1993). *Xiaoxue jiaoshi zhishi cidian* 小学教师知识词典

157

[encyclopedia of elementary school teachers' knowledge]. Shanghai: Shanghai Kexue Puji Chubanshe.
Li, X. Yunnan speaks easily understood Mandarin. (1992, May 21). *China Daily.*
Light, T. (1976). Comparative reading speeds with romanized and character texts. *Journal of the Chinese Language Teachers Association, 11*(1), 1-10.
Lin, J. (1993). *Education in post-Mao China.* Westport, CT: Praeger.
Lin, J. (1997). Policies and practices of bilingual education for the minorities in China. *Journal of Multilingual and Multicultural Development, 18*(3), 193-205.
Link, E. P. (1981). *Mandarin ducks and butterflies.* Berkeley: University of California Press.
Literacy classes help farmers to make money. (1994, April 19). *China Daily.*
Liu, I. M. (1988). Context effects on word/character naming: Alphabetic versus logographic languages. In I. M. Liu, H. C. Chen, & M. J. Chen (Eds.), *Cognitive aspects of the Chinese language, 1* (pp. 81-91). Hong Kong: Asian Research Service.
Liu, I. M., Chen, H. C., & Chen, M. J. (Eds.). (1988). *Cognitive Aspects of the Chinese Language, 1.* Hong Kong: Asian Research Service.
Lu, H. Thousands welcome new course. (1991, December 9). *China Daily.*
Lunyu 論語 [The analects of Confucius]. Qufu, PRC: Qufu Xian Wenwu Guanli Weiyuanhui.
Makie, R. (1980). *Literacy and revolution: The pedegogy of Paulo Freire.* New York: Continuum.
Makita, K. (1968). The rarity of reading disability in Japanese children. *American Journal of Orthopsychiatry, 38,* 599-614.
Manion, M. (1994). Survey research in the study of contemporary China: Learning from local samples. *The China Quarterly, 139,* 741-765.
Mann, V. A. (1988). Phonological awareness: A critical skill for beginning readers of alphabetic systems. In I. M. Liu, H. C. Chen, & M. J. Chen (Eds.), *Cognitive aspects of the Chinese language, 1* (pp. 109-118). Hong Kong: Asian Research Service.
Maps 'n facts. (1994). Novato, CA: Broderbund.
Martin, R. (1982) The socialization of children in China and on Taiwan: An analysis of elementary school textbooks. In P. G. Altbach, R. F. Arnove, & G. P. Kelly (Eds.), *Comparative education* (pp. 137-157). New York: Macmillan.
Mathes, P. G., Howard, J. K., Allen, S., & Fuchs, D. (1998). Peer-assisted learning strategies for first grade readers: Making early reading instruction more responsive to the needs of diverse learners. *Reading Research Quarterly, 33*(1), 62-95.
Mathews, M. M. (1966). *Teaching to read: Historically considered.* Chicago: University of Chicago Press.
Mathews, R. H. (1943). *Mathews' Chinese-English dictionary.* Cambridge: Harvard University Press.
Montaperto, R. N. & Henderson, J. (Eds.). (1979). *China's schools in flux.* White Plains, NY: M. E. Sharpe.
Morrow, L. M., Tracy, D. H., & Maxwell, C. M. (Eds.). (1995). *A survey of family literacy in the United States.* Newark, DE: International Reading Association.
Mosenthal, P. (1984). Defining reading program effectiveness: An ideological approach. *Poetics, 13,* 195-216.

158

Muth, K. D. (1989). *Children's comprehension of text: Research into practice.* Newark, DE: International Reading Association.

Nan, N. (1992). Sex discrimination in education. *Chinese Education, 25*(1), 44-47.

Nanjing students take to tutoring. (1990, October 18). *China Daily.*

Newmeyer, F. J. (Ed.). (1988). *Linguistics: The Cambridge survey, 1.* Cambridge: Cambridge University Press.

Norman, J. (1988). *Chinese.* Cambridge: Cambridge University Press.

Neuman, S. B. & Roskos, K. A. (Eds.). (1998). *Children achieving: Best practices in early literacy.* Newark, DE: International Reading Association.

Ogden, C. K. & Richards, I. A. (1949). *The meaning of meaning* (10th ed.). London: Kegan Paul. (Original work published 1923)

Ollila, L. O. & Mayfield, M. I. (1992). Home and school together: Helping beginning readers succeed. In S. J. Samuels & A. E. Farstrup (Eds.), *What research has to say about reading instruction* (2nd ed., pp.17-45). Newark, DE: International Reading Association.

Ono, K. (1989). *Chinese women in a century of revolution 1850-1950.* (J. A. Fogel, Ed.). Stanford, CA: Stanford University Press. (Original work published 1978)

Pan, L. (1983). *In search of old Shanghai.* Hong Kong: Joint Publishing.

Pay teachers their salaries. (1993, November 15). *China Daily.*

Pearson, P. D. (Ed.). (1984). *Handbook of reading research* (3rd ed.). New York: Longman.

Peng, T. H. (1984). *Hanyu Pinyin: Romanized Chinese phonetics.* Singapore: Times Books.

Perry, E. (1993). *Shanghai on strike: The politics of Chinese labor.* Stanford, CA: Stanford University Press.

Peterson, G. (1994). The struggle for literacy in post-revolutionary rural Guangdong. *The China Quarterly,* 926-943.

Petri, A. E. (1984). *Elementary education in the People's Republic of China.* (ERIC Document Reproduction Service No. ED 248 022)

Price, R. F. (1981). China: A problem of information? *Comparative Education Review, 23*(1), 85-92.

Pride, J. B. (1971). *The social meaning of language.* London: Oxford University Press.

Ramsey, R. S. (1987). *The languages of China.* Princeton: Princeton University Press.

Reforms of the Chinese written language. (1958). Peking: Foreign Languages Press.

The Republic of China yearbook 1994. (1993). Taipei: Government Information Office.

Rawski, E. (1979). *Education and popular literacy in Ch'ing China.* Ann Arbor: University of Michigan Press.

Reutzel, D. R., Oda, L. K., & Moore, B. H. (1989). Developing print awareness: The effect of three instructional approaches on kindergarteners' print awareness, reading readiness, and word reading. *Journal of Reading Behavior, 21*(3), 197-217.

Robins, R. H. (1988). Appendix. History of linguistics. In F. J. Newmeyer (Ed.), *Linguistics: The Cambridge survey, 1* (pp. 462-484). Cambridge: Cambridge University Press.

Robinson, J. C. (1986). Decentralization, money, and power: The case of people-

run schools in China. *Comparative Education Review, 30*(1), 73-88.
Robinson, J. C. (1991). Stumbling on two legs: Education and reform in China. *Comparative Education Review, 35*(1), 177-189.
Rohsenow, J. S. (1986). The second Chinese character simplification scheme. *International Journal of the Sociology of Language, 59*, 73-85.
Rosen, S. (1987). Survey research in the People's Republic of China: Some methodological problems. *Canadian and International Education, 16*(1), 211-220.
Rozin, P., Poritsky, S. & Sotsky, R. (1971). American children with reading problems can easily learn to read English represented by Chinese characters. *Science, 171* 1264-1267.
Ross, H. (1993). *China learns English: Language teaching and social change in the People's Republic of China.* New Haven, CT: Yale University Press.
Samuels, S. J. & Farstrup, A. E. (Eds.). (1992). *What research has to say about reading instruction.* (2nd ed.). Newark, DE: International Reading Association.
Seidenberg, M. (1985). The time course of phonological word activation in two writing systems. *Cognition, 19*, 1-30.
Senechal, M., Lefevre, J., Thomas, E. M., & Daley, K. E. (1998). Differential effects of home literacy experiences on the development of oral and written language. *Reading Research Quarterly, 33*(1), 96-116.
Serruys, P. L-M. (1962). *Survey of the Chinese language reform and the anti-illiteracy movement in communist China.* (Studies in Chinese Communist Terminology, 8). Berkeley: University of California.
Seybolt, P. J. & Chiang, G. K. (Eds.). (1979). *Language reform in China.* Armonk, NY: M.E. Sharpe.
Sheringham, M. (1984). Popularisation policies in Chinese education from the 1950s to the 1970s. *Comparative Education, 20*(1), 73-80.
Shih, V. Y. (1983). *The literary mind and the carving of dragons: A study of thought and pattern in Chinese literature.* Hong Kong: The Chinese University Press.
Shirk, S. L. (1979). Educational reform and political backlash: Recent changes in Chinese educational policy. *Comparative Education Review, 23*(2), 183-217.
Shu, H. & Anderson, R. C. (1997). Role of radical awareness in the character and word acquisition of Chinese children. *Reading Research Quarterly, 32*(1), 78-89.
Shuohua 说话 [Speaking] (Vol. 1). (1993). Beijing: Renmin Jiaoyu Chubanshe.
Sidel, R. (1982). Early childhood education in China: The impact of political change. *Comparative Education Review, 26*(1), 78-87.
Sinclair, J. (Ed.). (1987). *Collins Cobuild English language dictionary.* Glasgow: William Collins.
60% of 8-year-olds beaten by parents. (1992, December 14). *China Daily.*
Smith, F. (Ed.). (1973). *Psycholinguistics and reading.* New York: Holt, Rinehart &Winston.
Speaking in tongues. (1991, October 30). *China Daily.*
Some experiences in teaching English to primary one students. (1976). In S. M. Hu and E. Seifman (Eds.), *Toward a new world outlook: A documentary history of education in the People's Republic of China, 1949-1976* (pp. 277-279). New York: AMS Press. (Original work published 1972)
Spence, J. (1981). *The Gate of Heavenly Peace: The Chinese and their revolution*

160

1895-1980. New York: Viking.

Spence, J. (1984). *The memory palace of Matteo Ricci.* New York: Viking.

Spence, J. (1990). *The search for modern China.* New York: Norton.

Spence, J. (1992). *Chinese roundabout.* New York: Norton.

Spence, J. (1996). *God's Chinese son. The Taiping Heavenly Kingdom of Hong Xiuquan.* New York: Norton.

State again bans illegal school fees. (1993, October 4). *China Daily.*

Street, B. V. (1984). *Literacy in theory and practice.* Cambridge: Cambridge University Press.

Stubbs, M. (1980). *Language and literacy: The sociolinguistics of reading and writing.* London: Routledge & Kegan Paul.

Su, D. Simplified script is not so simple. (1991, June 9). *China Daily.*

Sutherland, M. B. (1987). Sex differences in education: An overview. *Comparative Education, 23*(1), 5-9.

Talented tots taught to excel by special scheme. (1992, November 28). *China Daily.*

Tang, L. (1979). A further discussion of the basic problems in the reform of Chinese writing. In P. J. Seybolt & G. K. Chiang (Eds.), *Language reform in China* (pp. 95-109). Armonk, NY: M. E. Sharpe. (Original work published 1957)

Taylor, I. & Taylor, M. M. (1995). *Writing and literacy in Chinese, Korean and Japanese.* Philadelphia: John Benjamins.

Teng, S. (1943). Chinese influence on the Western examination system. *Harvard Journal of Asiatic Studies, 7,* 267-312.

Till, B. (1984). *In search of old Nanking.* Hong Kong: Joint Publishing.

Tobin, J. J., Wu, D. Y. H., & Davidson, D. (1989). *Preschool in three cultures: Japan, China, and the United States.* New Haven, CT: Yale University Press.

Train more teachers-official. (1990, December, 10). *China Daily.*

Training network ups quality of teachers. (1990, December 1). *China Daily.*

Treiman, R. A., Baron, J., & Luk, K. (1981). Speech recoding in silent reading: A comparison of Chinese and English. *Journal of Chinese Linguistics, 9,* 116-125.

Tzeng, O., Hung, D., & Garro, L. (1978). Reading the Chinese characters: An information processing view. *Journal of Chinese Linguistics, 6,* 287-305.

Tzeng, O., Hung, D., & Wang, W. (1978). Speech recoding in reading Chinese characters. *Journal of Experimental Psychology, 3,* 621-630.

United in speaking 53 languages. (1991, December 4). *China Daily.*

Vaughan, J. (1993). Early childhood education in China. *Childhood Education* (summer), 196-200.

Wagner, D. A. (1990). Literacy assessment in the third world: An overview and proposed schema for survey use. *Comparative Education Review, 34*(1), 112-138.

Walker, G. (1984). 'Literacy' and 'reading' in a Chinese language program. *Journal of the Chinese Language Teachers Association, 19*(1), 67-84.

Wang, J. (1996). On the modernization of the Chinese language: Bilingualism and digraphia in China. *Journal of the Chinese Language Teachers Association, 31*(3), 10-14.

Wang, R. Schooling helps use human resources. (1990, November 29). *China Daily.*

Wang, S. (1984). *Lu Xun: A biography.* Beijing: Foreign Languages Press.

Wang, S. H. (1994). Speech at the inaugural conference of the Shanghai primary and secondary schools curriculum and teaching materials reform committee. *Chinese Education and Society, 27*(1), 13-42.

Watkins, D. A. & Biggs, J. B. (Eds.). (1996). *The Chinese learner: Cultural, psychological, and contextual influences.* Hong Kong: Comparative Education Research Centre, University of Hong Kong.

Weber, L. (1979). Early childhood education. In R. N. Montaperto & J. Henderson (Eds.), *China's schools in flux* (pp. 124-134). White Plains, NY: M. E. Sharpe.

Wei, J. (1979). From the "National Language" movement to standardization of the Chinese language. In P. J. Seybolt & G. K. Chiang (Eds.), *Language reform in China* (pp. 288-299). Armonk, NY: M. E. Sharpe. (Original work published 1959)

Wen, H. (1979). The written language must be reformed. In P. J. Seybolt & G. K. Chiang (Eds.), *Language reform in China* (pp. 349-354). Armonk, NY: M. E. Sharpe. (Original work published 1973)

Whyte, M. K. (1996). The Chinese family and economic development: Obstacle or Engine? *Economic Development and Cultural Change, 45*(1), 1-30.

Wieger, L. (1965). *Chinese characters: Their origin, etymology, history, classification and signification* (2nd ed.). New York: Dover. (Original work published 1927)

Wigfield, A. & Asher, S. R. (1984). Social and motivational influences on reading. In P. D. Pearson (Ed.), *Handbook of reading research* (pp. 423-451). New York: Longman.

Williams, C. A. S. (1976). *Outlines of Chinese symbolism and art motives.* New York: Dover. (Original work published 1941)

Willinsky, J. (1990). *The new literacy: Redefining reading and writing in the schools.* New York: Routledge.

Wolf, M. (1985). *Revolution postponed: Women in contemporary China.* Stanford, CA: Stanford University Press.

Wrenn, J. J. (1975). Popularization of Putonghua. *Journal of Chinese Linguistics, 3*(2/3), 221-227.

Wu, J. R. (Ed.). (1985). *The Pinyin Chinese-English dictionary.* New York: John Wiley.

Wu, Y. (1958). Report on the current tasks of reforming the written language and the draft scheme for a Chinese phonetic alphabet. In *Reform of the Chinese written language,* (pp. 30-59). Peking: Foreign Languages Press.

Wu, Y. (1979). Push forward with the work of writing reform in the script of seeking truth by verifying facts. In P. J. Seybolt & G. K. Chiang (Eds.), *Language Reform in China* (pp. 300-307). Armonk, NY: M. E. Sharpe. (Original work published 1959).

Wu, Yuanli. (Ed.). (1973). *China: A handbook.* New York: Praeger.

Xi, M. Spread of non-standard characters. (1991, October 31). *China Daily.*

Xi, M. Only a collective effort can solve the problems in the education system. (1994, March 17). *China Daily.*

Xie, L. *Fantizi* a fantasy for foreigners. (1989, December 4). *China Daily.*

Xie, L. Basic education to be secured for children. (1991, December 6). *China Daily.*

Xu, M. (1979). A solicited letter. In P. J. Seybolt & G. K. Chiang (Eds.), *Language reform in China* (pp. 199-201). Armonk, NY: M. E. Sharpe. (Original work published 1957)

162

Yamadori, A. (1988). Writing and hemispheric coordination. *Aphasiology*, 2, 427-432.

Yin, B. & Baldauf, R. B., Jr. (1990). Language reform in spoken Chinese. *Journal of Multilingual and Multicultural Development*, 11(4), 279-290.

Yin, B. & Felley, M. (1990). *Chinese romanization: Pronunciation and orthography.* Beijing: Sinolingua.

Yin, W. & Butterworth, B. (1992). Deep and surface dyslexia in Chinese. In H. C. Chen, & O. Tzeng (Eds.), *Language processing in Chinese* (pp. 349-366). Amsterdam, NL: Elsevier.

Yu, S. Kids' schooling a team effort. (1992, June 30). *China Daily*, p. 6.

Yuwen 语文 [Chinese language] Vol. 1. (1990). Beijing: Renmin Jiaoyu Chubanshe

Yun, Z. (1994). Toward the schools of the future: An exploration of primary and secondary models of education. *Chinese Education and Society*, 27(1), 8-12.

Zhan, W. In China, English is a mark of success. (1990, December 6). *China Daily*, p. 6.

Zhang, Xia. Ending illiteracy among rural women. (1994, July 4). *China Daily*.

Zhang, Xin. Teacher shortage threatens colleges. (1991, May 6). *China Daily*, p. 4.

Zhang, Xiruo (1979). Resolutely promote the standard vernacular based on Peking pronunciation. In P. J. Seybolt & G. K. Chiang (Eds.), *Language reform in China* (pp. 65-77). Armonk, NY: M. E. Sharpe. (Original work published 1955)

Zhou, E. (1979). The immediate tasks in writing reform. In P. J. Seybolt & G. K. Chiang (Eds.), *Language reform in China* (pp. 228-243). Armonk, NY: M. E. Sharpe. (Original work published 1958)

Zhou, Y. (1986). Modernization of the Chinese language. *International Journal of the Sociology of Language*, 59, 7-23.

Zhu, Y. Linguists want to stop 'pollution' of Chinese. (1991, June 7). *China Daily*.

163

Index

164

166

167

168

Shirk, S. L., 51
Shu, H. & Anderson, R., 8, 117
Shuohua, 118
Sidel, R., 8
Sinclair, J, 127
Singapore, 135
slates, 68, 71, 77, 79, 82, 94, 96, 101
Smith, F., 91
sociolinguistics, 8, 13, 16, 18, 20, 79, 135
social mobility, 3, 17, 35, 58, 130, 134, 136
"Some Experiences," 101
speech community, 6, 11, 19, 81
Spence, J., 7, 22
standard language, iii, 4, 6, 9, 11, 14-19, 21, 25, 27, 30, 35, 36, 128, 130, 133-135, 139, 143; pronunciation, iii, 5, 26, 29, 36, 38, 76, 82, 84, 86, 115; scripts, 9, 37, 38, 114, 115, 134, 139; vocabulary, 5, 78-81; written text, 28, 136, *see also* Guoyu, Putonghua, and prestige
"State Bans," 57
State Council, 31, 33, 37
State Education Commission, 49, 55
stories, 70
Street, B., 131
Stubbs, M., 6
Su, D., 34
Subeiren, 20
syllables, 9, 19, 23, 24, 27-29, 36, 66, 67, 70-72, 76-82, 90, 93, 94, 97-101, 103-107, 110, 119-122, 124, 129, 139; syllabic pronunciation, 90, 91
syllabary, 23, 91, 148, 149

Taiwan, 7, 15, 16, 20, 26, 29, 90, 117, 132, 135, 147, 149, 150
"Talented Tots," 112
Tang, Lan, 36
tape recorders, 50, 81
Taylor, I. & Taylor, M., 5, 6, 110, 141, 149
teacher, iv, v, 5, 6, 9, 35, 37, 58, 60, 62, 63, 65-125, 127, 129, 134, 140; compensation, 6, 52-54, 57, 63, 140; elementary school, 44, 46, 47, 49-51, 53-58, 131, 135; kindergarten, 59, 61; middle school, 134; training, 25, 36, 55, 56, 57; treatment of, 6, 54
Teachers' Day, 54
Television University, 57
tests, Hanyu Pinyin, 103-106, 119-122; Chinese characters, 119-122;

Putonghua, 122-124
textbooks, 49, 55, 113, 115-119; presentation of material, 60, 114, 116, 117
Tiananmen Square, 1, 50
tianzige, 113, 115, 149
Tobin, J. J., Wu, D. Y. H., & Davidson, D., 8, 61
tone, 9, 28, 29, 36, 67, 68, 70, 78-81, 93, 94, 96, 105, 106, 110, 111, 114; tone sandhi, 79
tracking, 51
train drill, 72, *see also* games
"Training Network," 55
"Train More Teachers," 55
Trigault, Nicholas, 22
tuition, 57
tutor, 60
Tzeng, O., Hung, D., & Garro, L., 7
Tzeng, O. Hung, D., & Wang, W., 7

UNESCO, 2, 127
"United in Speaking 53 Languages," 35
urban areas, 3-5, 27, 44, 46, 49, 51, 57, 59, 61, 62, 66, 95, 102, 110, 112, 118, 125, 140
uniforms (school), 49

vernacular, 5, 36, 38, 127-129, 133, 135; literature, 23, 26, 27
visual aids, 69, 77
vocabulary, 16, 18; learning, 68, 70, 71, 75, 78-81, 103, 110, 111, 115-117
von Humboldt, 99
vowels, 19, 67-69, 71, 78, 82, 91, 104, 147, 148

Wade-Giles romanization, 9, 22, 66, 149, 151, 152
Wang Zhao, 23
Wang, R., 141
Weber, L., 8
Wei, J. 36
Wenyan, 23, 24, 27, 39, 132, 150
whole-word approach, 90
Whyte, M. K., 131
Wieger, L., 7
Wolf, M., 118
word formation, 83, 84, 90-96, 99-101, 103, 105-107
word processing, 86, 142
Women's script, 133, 134

writing Hanyu Pinyin, 83-127; Chinese
Characters, 109-125
Wu, J. R., 99
Wu Yuzhang, 8, 29, 30, 34-36, 107
Wu dialect group, 13, 14, 16-20, 23, 75, 106,
128, 134, 135, 150

Xi, M., 115
Xie, L., 141
Xiamen, 12, 17, 18, 20, 135
Xiang dialect group, 12-14
xiaopengyou, 69, 96
Xu, M., 36

Yamadori, A., 7
Yin, B. & Baldauf, R. B., 8, 35, 56
Yin, W. & Butterworth, B., 92
Yizhongxin School, v, 47-55, 57, 63, 66, 69,
70, 72, 77, 81-83, 87, 92, 93, 101, 102,
104-107, 109, 119, 139, see also
neighborhood school
Yu, S., 49, 59, 60
Yunnan Province, 128
Yuwen, 46, 47, 57, 119, 122, 150
Yuwen, 116

Zhan, W., 102
Zhang Xia, 130
Zhang Xin, 55
Zhang Xiruo, 56
Zhejiang Normal University, 134
Zhejiang Province, 34
Zhihu, 90, 92, 93, 150, see also phonics
Zhuang nationality, 128
Zhou Enlai, 37, 38, 43, 46
Zhou Youguang, 8, 24, 31, 33, 36, 124
Zhu, Y., 134
Zhuyin Fuhao, 25, 150, see also Guoyin Zimu